Connecting *the* Dots

· ·

A Hope-Inspired Life

Jake Owensby

WestBow
PRESS
A DIVISION OF THOMAS NELSON

Copyright © 2012 by Jake Owensby.

All rights reserved. No part of this book may be used or reproduced by any means, graphic, electronic, or mechanical, including photocopying, recording, taping or by any information storage retrieval system without the written permission of the publisher except in the case of brief quotations embodied in critical articles and reviews.

WestBow Press books may be ordered through booksellers or by contacting:

WestBow Press
A Division of Thomas Nelson
1663 Liberty Drive
Bloomington, IN 47403
www.westbowpress.com
1-(866) 928-1240

Because of the dynamic nature of the Internet, any web addresses or links contained in this book may have changed since publication and may no longer be valid. The views expressed in this work are solely those of the author and do not necessarily reflect the views of the publisher, and the publisher hereby disclaims any responsibility for them.

Any people depicted in stock imagery provided by Thinkstock are models, and such images are being used for illustrative purposes only.

Certain stock imagery © Thinkstock.

ISBN: 978-1-4497-5798-4 (hc)
ISBN: 978-1-4497-5797-7 (hc)
ISBN: 978-1-4497-5796-0 (e)

Library of Congress Control Number: 2012911552

Printed in the United States of America

WestBow Press rev. date: 6/27/2012

Contents

Preface		ix
Introduction		xi
1	Hope: Trusting God to Connect the Dots	1
2	Finding Happiness	17
3	A Life that Matters	33
4	Hope Amid the Weeds	51
5	Picturing Eternity: Heaven and Hell	64
6	Anger and Forgiveness: Reconnecting the Dots	84
7	Fear and Hope	97
Bibliography		113

To Joy, Andrew, Meredith, and Patrick

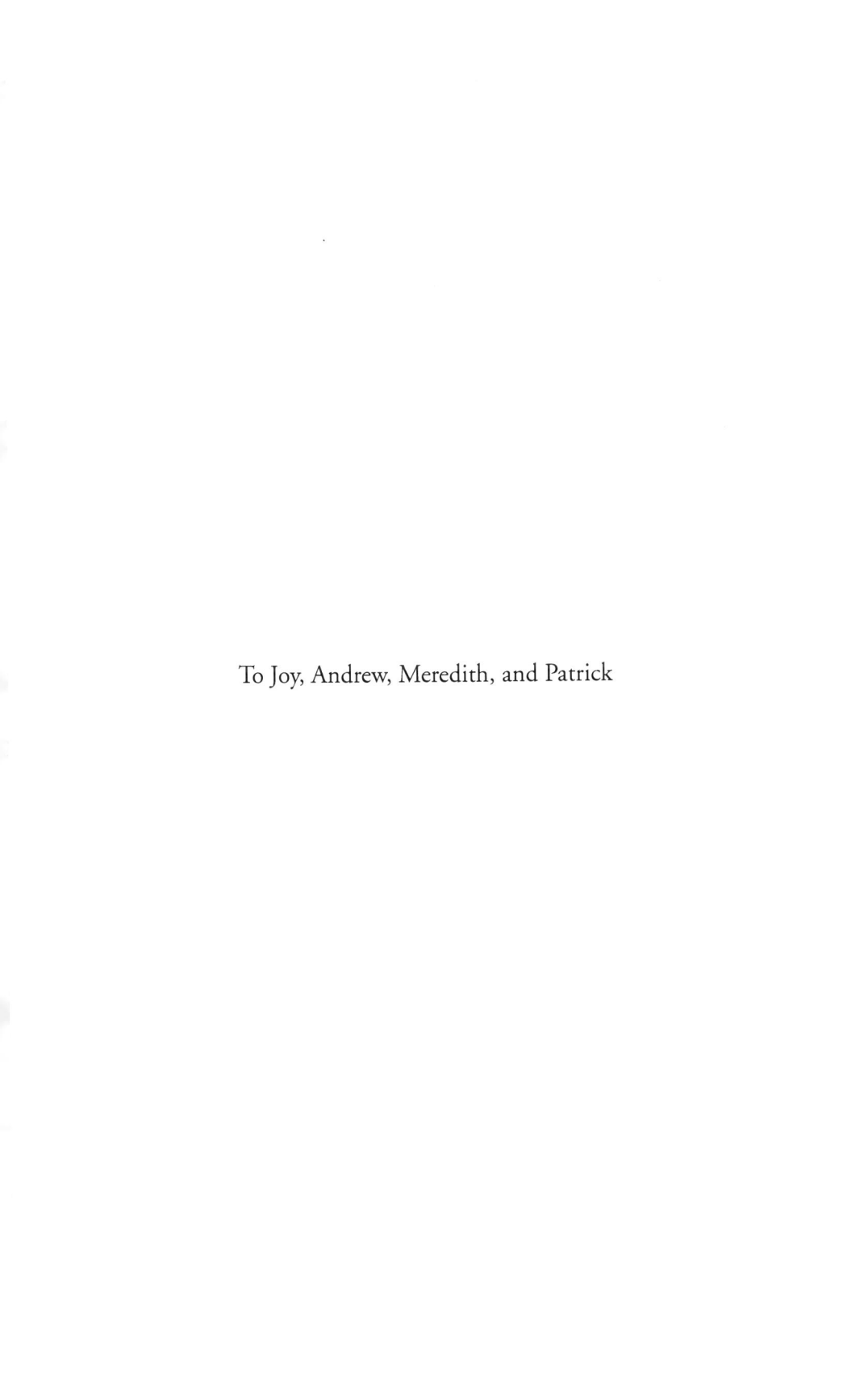

The Lord will keep your going out and your coming in from this time forth and forevermore.

—Psalm 121:8

Preface

Your life matters, and it matters on an infinite and eternal scale. That may sound like a bold claim. Maybe you spend most of your day behind a desk, chauffeuring children, or repeating one of a thousand ordinary routines. Nothing about your daily life seems world-changing or history-making to you. Perhaps a life-crushing loss or a humiliating setback has left you feeling that your world is irreparably broken. Chronic illness or a stalled career could make you wonder whether you have anything truly significant to offer. You may have reached the pinnacle of success, yet you find yourself wondering, "Is this all there is?"

Nevertheless, your life matters. That is the core message of Christian hope. This book is devoted to helping its readers not only understand the concept of hope, but more importantly, to drawing upon hope as a powerful force that inspires our daily lives. Christian hope is much more than merely wishful thinking or a positive attitude. Optimism in all its forms places its bets on what we humans can accomplish. By contrast, hope is rooted in what Christ has already achieved on the cross and what God promises to accomplish for us in the future.

God connects the dots of our lives. By God's sovereign grace, what we do makes sense and has significance for eternity. We are part of a larger picture that, without us, is incomplete, and that God himself will bring to completion. The details of that larger picture remain largely obscured, yet the promise of the picture inspires us to move forward. The presence of the Holy Spirit in our lives acts as a guarantee of that promise and sustains our trust in it.

To help instill hope in my readers, I begin this book with a discussion of how God gets involved in our daily lives. We then turn to a discussion of true happiness and how to achieve it. The next chapters tackle how we can make an eternal difference in ordinary life and how, as followers of Jesus, we should confront evil in this world. In the fifth chapter, I discuss eternal life (heaven and hell) as a sketch of the big picture in which our daily lives are situated. The final two chapters address the pastoral implications of hope. Many of us have to work at coping with anger, learning to forgive, and overcoming fear. These final chapters explain how to draw on God's presence and power to let go of resentment and bitterness, and to replace timidity with boldness.

There are many fine translations of the Bible, but all passages cited in this book are drawn from the English Standard Version, unless otherwise noted; I have also relied heavily on the New Revised Standard Version, the New International Version, and the Psalter as it is rendered in *The Book of Common Prayer*.

Many people have played a part in getting this book into its final form. I would like to specifically acknowledge a few of them. Friends and colleagues agreed to read drafts of chapters at various stages. Their comments and encouragement were invaluable. Mark Galli, Brad Drell, Chuck Alley, Ed Little, and Dan Martins each gave me much to think about and solid advice with the manuscript. Cheryl White endured several versions of this manuscript and offered her time and insight over countless cups of coffee.

The staff members of St. Mark's Cathedral are dear friends and colleagues of mine. Their excellent ministry made it possible for me to concentrate my energies on this project. The good people of St. Mark's Cathedral helped me to develop my ideas by allowing me the privilege of preaching and teaching in their midst. I am especially grateful to my administrative supports, Liz Montelepre and Bess Maxwell.

Finally, and above all, my wife Joy has been with me during this project, from start to finish, serving as my soundboard, my editor, and my chief encourager. I am blessed to have so many wonderful people in my life.

INTRODUCTION

We all want to do something that matters. Believing that our actions make a significant contribution, that our commitments to other people will make a difference in their lives, or that our devotion to causes will make the world a better place keeps us moving forward in life, heading somewhere, seeming to accomplish something important. And yet, sometimes, life makes no sense. Life feels like just one thing after another, an endless series of meetings and project deadlines, chauffeuring kids, shopping for groceries, and paying bills. Or worse, life seems to fly apart at the seams: your marriage is slipping away, you've lost your job, your kids are distant and self-destructive, your parent no longer recognizes you because of the ravages of dementia, and a loved one dies.

We persevere through monotonous times and through heart-rending times. What keeps us going is the conviction that, despite appearances, life really does make sense, that it all fits together somehow and is heading toward some climax that will show us there is a point to all we have endured. The belief that everything will make sense inspires us to keep going, to take risks, to face adversity, and to overcome setbacks.

Christians call this inspiration "hope." Hope inspires us to take on each day with a sense of purpose because we trust that God will connect the dots of our lives, even if we don't see just how he will accomplish that. Think about it this way: making sense of your life is like doing one of those connect-the-dots puzzles. You know the kind I am talking about. On a sheet in front of you (sometimes on a kid's menu at a family restaurant), you see what look like a meaningless jumble of numbered points, but when you draw lines between the points in the correct sequence, a picture slowly emerges of a clown, a car, or some other familiar object.

Eventually, we all want to connect the dots of our lives. We want life to make sense. And so you look back on the past events of your life up to the present and try to discern how one thing led to another to get you where you are today, often by telling the story of your own life. You might tell the story to yourself. You might share it with a friend or a counselor. But each of us shapes his or her life into a story with a sense of direction and an ending in which everything from the past culminates in the here and now.

There is just one problem. We can only connect the dots by looking backward. We live life forward; the future is an unfinished picture. To do anything at all, to take the next step in life, we have to believe that all of our dots are somehow connected. We have to trust in something, in someone, to complete the picture. Some people trust in their own ingenuity or intelligence. Others believe in karma, destiny, fate, or luck. None of these things is the same as hope, at least not the Christian meaning of the word. Hope is the inspiration we gain from trusting in God's promise to connect the dots of our lives through his son, Jesus Christ. As the apostle Paul puts it in Romans, hope wells up from our belief that "in all things God works for the good of those who love him" (Romans 8:28 NIV).

To get your head around the idea of hope, consider for a moment its opposite, despair. The existentialist philosopher Albert Camus retold the Greek myth of Sisyphus to illustrate his idea of the hopelessness of human life. The gods punished Sisyphus by sentencing him to push a boulder up a hill for eternity. Each time the boulder approached the summit, it rolled back down the hill again, and Sisyphus would have to repeat the entire process. In other words, nothing that Sisyphus did amounted to anything. His aspirations would always turn to dust, and his toil would always be fruitless. And most devastating of all, he knew it. That is why Camus stated that the first philosophical question is whether or not to commit suicide. What is the point of life when it all comes to nothing? When the dots never connect?

Sometimes the hardships of life can make us feel like Sisyphus. Life takes many unexpected turns, and some of them feel like Sisyphus's boulder rolling over us: a divorce, a career setback, an unwelcome diagnosis, the sickness of a parent, or the learning and social challenges of a child. Perhaps it all seemed to be coming together before, but now it looks like meaningless jumble. It is not just that you have to figure out how you slipped or lost your grip this one time; the notion that this is all that will ever happen, that the boulder will always roll back down the hill, starts to creep up on you.

Let us return to the connect-the dots puzzle. If you cannot connect the dots by yourself, that is when you need hope to be able to move at all. You need to trust in something that will inspire you to keep drawing, even if they do not seem to be composing a picture. Camus did not believe in an afterlife or a deity who was working on his behalf. He concluded that the only hope that exists is to admit that there is no ultimate hope. All that matters is having the strength to affirm the value of one's own existence in the face of the brute fact that nothing really matters in the long run. He believed we should just go for it with all we have, because this life is all that we've got. We must act as though what we do will work out.

Some people may be able to motivate themselves temporarily with wishful thinking, with what they know to be no nothing more than a lovely fiction. But, as I will discuss at length in this book, we have an inextinguishable yearning for more than this. We want our lives to matter eternally. Camus suggests that we draw the strength to keep living and loving and making a contribution to the world from our own strength of belief that what we do matters. In contrast, Christians insist that it is not the strength of our own capacity to hope that matters. On the contrary, we recognize that it is the strength of the thing upon which we place our hope that really matters. To use a familiar example, if I am dangling from a root at the edge of a cliff, I can be the strongest man in the world, yet I will still fall if the root is too flimsy to hold my weight. Jesus teaches us to move forward in trusting in him. He can bear our weight. He will connect the dots.

Jesus is God's Messiah. He has come to set things right. On the cross, he set us right with the Father. But he is not finished yet. He will return to connect the dots in the new heaven and the new earth. In the meantime, he tells us to go about doing the work he has given us. He says, "It is like a man going on a journey, when he leaves home and puts his slaves in charge, each with his work, and commands the doorkeeper to be on the watch" (Mark 13:35). In other words, we may not see exactly how all of the dots will connect. At times, we might see nothing more than a chaotic mess. No picture seems ready to emerge—at least no picture we'd want to post on life's refrigerator door. Keep scribbling dots anyway! Trust Jesus to connect them.

Some Christians think of Jesus' work primarily in terms of getting into heaven. See if this sounds familiar to you. Heaven is a paradise into which worthy souls fly after death. There are entrance requirements. Some say that you must proclaim Jesus Christ as your Lord and Savior before drawing your last breath in order to enter heaven's gates. Others say that you have to believe in Jesus and do good works. Still others think that Jesus gives us a last chance, just after we die, to put our faith in him. Today, it is increasingly common to believe that death is the only requirement to entering heaven. This is called universalism.

If you think of heaven as a distant place which you will inhabit following this life, then you may see life on earth as something you leave behind. Perhaps you consider this life to be a vale of tears, nothing more than a test for the next life. But the more joyful and contented you are on this planet, the less likely you are to see departure as desirable. This is something you may hesitate to share with your pastor. In any event, if you see life as something that will be left behind, then everything around you is tainted with the aroma of impermanence. It all goes away; it will be water under the bridge of eternity, celestial spilled milk. It does not matter because it does not last.

But proper understanding of the work of Jesus Christ is the opposite of that. Hope is based on our belief in life after this life, but it looks nothing like the picture of going to heaven sketched above. Christian teaching laces this life with eternal significance; the Bible teaches us that God will redeem his creation. It is more consistent with the Bible to think of Jesus exercising his gracious reign over a new heaven and a new earth at his second coming. Consider this passage:

> Then I saw a new heaven and a new earth, for the first heaven and the first earth had passed away, and the sea was no more. And I saw the holy city, new Jerusalem, coming down out of heaven from God, prepared as a bride adorned for her husband. And I heard a loud voice from the throne saying, "Behold, the dwelling place of God is with man. He will dwell with them, and they will be his people, and God

> himself will be with them as their God. He will wipe away every tear from their eyes, and death shall be no more, neither shall there be mourning, nor crying, nor pain anymore, for the former things have passed away."
> —Revelation 21:1–4

Jesus promises to return. He does not come to eradicate the earth. Instead, he comes to be with us in a renewed heaven and earth. When God is with us, everything changes. Right now, God's presence is intermittent and obscure. Hope is relying on the promise that one day, God will be unceasingly present, with dazzling clarity. Sorrow and death will evaporate forever in his presence. The forces that seem to reduce life to a scattered jumble of dots will be defeated once and for all. God will connect all the dots into a breathtaking picture.

In the Bible, there are remarkably appealing images of life after life as an era of justice and peace. Take, for instance, Isaiah's words:

> The wolf shall dwell with the lamb, and the leopard shall lie down with the young goat, and the calf and the lion and the fattened calf together; and a little child shall lead them. The cow and the bear shall graze; their young shall lie down together; and the lion shall eat straw like the ox. The nursing child shall play over the hole of the cobra, and the weaned child shall put his hand on the adder's den. They shall not hurt or destroy in all my holy mountain; for the earth shall be full of the knowledge of the Lord as the waters cover the sea.
> —Isaiah 11:6–9

The prophet envisions a time in which there is no longer a distinction between predator and prey. Human beings go about their lives as vulnerable as little children without the slightest fear of injury.

The key is to remember that the new heaven and new earth is not so much a distant place as a future time when God will be perpetually present in the midst of his creation. Some people seem to think that the goal of life is getting into heaven, and that God acts merely as a kind of gatekeeper you cannot avoid dealing with during the admission phase of the afterlife, but once you have gone through the pearly gates and found your way to the great wedding feast, it hardly matters whether or not you talk to the host ever again. Focusing in this way on the afterlife as a place to enter can lead one to believe the point of life is achieving a perpetual state of joy and eternal freedom from sorrow and pain; God then becomes a mere means to the eternal comfort we really seek. In contrast, the Bible teaches us repeatedly that to be in God's holy presence should be our deepest, most abiding desire.

The Psalmist says, "One thing have I asked of the Lord, that will I seek after: that I may dwell in the house of the Lord all the days of my life, to gaze upon the beauty of the Lord and to inquire in his temple" (Psalm 27:4). The Psalm does not say, "I want to dwell in the house of the Lord; it has a lovely view and comfortable furniture." Neither does it say, "I want to house-sit in paradise while God is gone." The Psalmist's desire, and our enduring desire, is "to gaze upon the beauty of the Lord." His presence is the game changer. When he is present—and only when he is present—we will dwell in a heaven and earth transformed by his presence. The lives that we now lead will be redeemed and made whole. As the prophet Joel says, "I will restore to you the years that the swarming locust has eaten" (Joel 2:25). In Jesus Christ, God will connect the dots.

Jesus teaches his disciples to engage the world we inhabit guided, sustained, and strengthened by hope. He said, "Seek first the kingdom of God" (Matthew 6:33). The apostle Paul spoke about having the mind of Christ (1 Corinthians 2:16; Philippians 2:4–11). Jesus teaches us that waiting expectantly for the new heaven and the new earth leads us to make a difference on earth, in his name. We serve the kingdom of heaven by living a certain way at school, at work, in the community, and in our neighborhoods.

The guiding principle of this book is that to hope for the new heaven and the new earth does not mean to yearn for a place beyond here. Instead, a hope-inspired life draws vigor and joy by engaging the messiness of present life with the expectation that through us, God is about to do something in the world we inhabit. A hope-inspired life acknowledges the conflicts, contradictions, and brokenness of our present lives, yet sees them as the unfinished picture that God will eventually complete. This life is not the whole picture. It is a great picture of God's kingdom in the making. Not only is there life after this life, but also, all of history culminates in the return of the crucified and risen Christ. He will establish perfect justice, heal every wound, and eliminate death and suffering once and for all. But above all, he will dwell among his people. The new heaven and the new earth, in other words, is shorthand for the perfect presence of God. Being hopeful is yearning for God's presence as our hidden treasure, our pearl of great price. We dwell on earth waiting expectantly for his coming. In the meantime, God has a plan for his creation, and Jesus' followers have the joy and privilege of being active participants in making that plan a reality. For hopeful followers of Jesus, these truths are the lenses through which we see our daily lives and discern the good that we can do in Christ's name, in every situation.

Thus, getting into heaven is not the top priority, not because heaven should take a back seat to earthly concerns, but because talk about getting into heaven frequently contains an unbiblical understanding of heaven and earth. For some, heaven represents an escape from the world. Basing our hope on a flight to heaven means being forgetful of the here and now. This is not what Jesus taught us. His instruction to seek the kingdom comes right in the middle of the Sermon on the Mount (Matthew 5–7). This sermon is filled with very earthly issues, like forgiving those who hurt you, handling your money for holy purposes, and expressing sexual desires in love instead of lust. Seeking the kingdom of God involves living on this earth as if God himself were your King, in preparation for the day when that really will be the case.

Similarly, waiting expectantly for the new heaven and new earth means believing that we cannot live perfect lives or create perfect societies. God is sovereign and will restore our broken world to the goodness and beauty he originally intended for us. He will actually dwell among us as our King. But this is not to say that we can ignore hunger and prejudice and violence today because Daddy will eventually take care of it. We anticipate his coming by letting his vision guide our work with the poor, the lonely, the lost, and the helpless.

Jesus did not have in mind for us to neglect the earth for the sake of a distant heaven. Neither did he teach us to expect earth to be heaven. Some ministries which focus on social justice neglect to preach Jesus as our Savior from sin, death, and judgment. In fact, they equate the Gospel of Christ with the work of feeding the hungry, dismantling oppressive laws, and overcoming human prejudice. They interpret the work of salvation in largely earthly terms, and, perhaps unwittingly, they give the impression that political action and economic engineering will heal our world's ills. At the risk of being unfair, it almost seems that they would dispense with God if we could establish perfect justice without him. Justice, not God himself, is their pearl of great price. As a result, they dream of structuring earthly institutions and educating human hearts in a way that eradicates the evils of what are, in fact, the intractable effects of the fall.

Others, in a different way, expect to find heaven on earth. Because they rightly understand God as one who lavishly blesses his creatures, they focus almost exclusively on seeking blessings for themselves and those whom they hold dear. According to this view, health and wealth come to those who believe and pray faithfully. But they are left unable to explain how Paul could say that he participated in the very life of Christ by sharing in his sufferings. From the perspective of these people, suffering is an intrusion on a life of blessing. They cannot see how suffering could be a means of spiritual growth because, in their own way, they believe that this earth can be heaven.

In this book, I suggest that followers of Jesus are God's hope-inspired agents in this world, and that our hope wells up from our trust that God will eventually connect the dots of life. In the first chapter, I will discuss God's sovereignty and our free will. I explain that God has a completed picture in mind, and human beings play a role in crafting that picture. Specifically, I shall address how God exercises his will and implements his plan for us, yet still leaves room for us to make choices and take responsibility for them.

To wait for God to connect the dots of his creation picture means that we shall not know complete fulfillment in this life. But that does not mean that God consigns us to misery, nor that we should resign ourselves to a life of perpetual frustration and disappointment; on the contrary. Chapter Two explains how being hope-inspired brings a present joy which can never be achieved by those who seek their greatest good and ultimate happiness in the finite comforts, achievements, and status of this world.

We all want to do something that matters with our lives. In contemporary America, people assume that some careers are more significant than others, so they seek to validate their lives through their career choices. Many look to justify their lives through their achievements or through financial legacies of some kind. But believing that God ultimately connects the dots helps us to realize that following the will of God is what makes our lives matter. Chapter Three discusses two ways to make meaningful contributions. First, we can learn to exercise wisdom in our ordinary lives to make inroads for the kingdom of heaven in our corner of the planet. Second, we can commit ourselves to prayer, understanding that God does much of his work through the prayers of his Son's followers.

Chapter Four spends some time looking honestly at the earth we inhabit; we look plainly at God's fallen creation. There is good and evil around us. Jesus himself teaches us to love, to forgive, and to refuse to pass judgment. Many Christians assume that the use of force in responding to evil violates Jesus' teaching, and above all, his example. This chapter argues that Christian love can at times take forceful measures in confronting evil. As hope-inspired people, we acknowledge that God is the ultimate judge of good and evil, yet we must actively persevere in our struggle against evil.

If we were creatures merely of this earth, then the choices we make and the life-habits we cultivate would die with us. But we are heavenly-minded; this means that everything we do has an eternal trajectory. This life leads beyond itself to the next life. What we do points toward a final destination. In Chapter Five, I explain how we worship what we choose to be our highest good, and that what we worship as our highest good shapes all the lesser choices of our lives, and in fact, sets us on an eternal path. I also discuss heaven and hell as the recurring patterns of worship which we embrace during our time on earth.

The sixth and seventh chapters turn to practical matters in daily living. Chapter Six explains how hope in God's ultimate reign transforms our hearts. We can leave anger behind us when we genuinely believe that God's mercy and God's justice complete the dots. Forgiveness, not anger, has the last word in a hope-inspired life. Finally, Chapter Seven outlines how hope overcomes fear. Fear is a common companion for many of us. While reasonable fear is a helpful tool in various circumstances, fear can also drain the joy out of life. Trusting in God's sovereignty replaces the burden of fear with creative energy, excitement, and positive urgency about getting on with our next steps.

CHAPTER ONE

HOPE: TRUSTING GOD TO CONNECT THE DOTS

Life is like an elaborate, unfinished, connect-the-dots puzzle. We do not initially see how all the dots will be joined together. We may glimpse bits and pieces of a picture, but there are many ill-fitting fragments. To make matters even more complicated, billions of dots are obviously missing. Someone will add them later. Our stomachs churn and our hearts race when we wonder how our kids will turn out, if our loved ones will return from the war in one piece or at all, whether this rough patch in our marriage will end in divorce, and what the results of our medical test will be. We do not know with any reliability what will happen next, so we worry about how the picture will turn out in the end. For instance, we believe that God wants children to be happy and well fed, yet many of them are abused and starving. It is hard to take the next step if we believe we will end up with a picture full of sorrow, disappointment, and failure. In fact, we wonder whether a coherent picture will emerge at all, or if we will be left with nothing more than chaotic scribbling. To follow Jesus is to take the next step in life, trusting that God will somehow connect the dots. Hope inspires us to keep moving forward because we believe that God is fashioning a breathtaking picture through our faithful, obedient actions. He is not finished yet, but he is at work.

To put this another way, following Jesus means believing that God gets involved in our earthly lives in a decisive way. He is not just a distant spectator; he is a passionate one. God is by your side and he has your back. He is the creator of fields and skies, the author of oceans and galaxies, the mover of tides and tectonic plates; he knows the number of hairs on your head and he grieves when a sparrow falls. Even more astonishingly, we Christians say that God is out in front of us. He guards us and guides us. He has a vision for our lives. He will make that vision a reality when we rely upon him. Christians sometimes describe God's involvement in our lives by saying that God has a plan, and that his will governs the universe. In this book, I use the metaphor of connect-the-dots puzzles. God connects the dots of our lives—and of his whole creation—into a meaningful, beautiful picture. Theologians call this the sovereignty of God.

God's sovereignty gives us hope. Even when life seems to be flying apart at the seams, our trust that God will connect the dots motivates us to take the next step. What puzzles many is the apparent contradiction between God's sovereignty and our freedom to choose. Some thinkers assume that if God connects the dots, then we must not have any freedom to make choices about the shape of our lives. Before we dwell more fully on God's vision for our lives as the source of our hope, let's turn first to a discussion of how God connects the dots, yet still leaves room for us to make choices and take responsibility for our actions.

Suffering and Sovereignty

Any suggestion that God connects the dots here on earth runs into trouble right away. After all, rotten things happen. Natural disasters like earthquakes, tsunamis, hurricanes, and droughts cause terrible human suffering. Some interpret these natural disasters as God's punishment for sin. God is sovereign, they say. If something happens, God made it happen. Following this line of thinking, God can only be good if those who suffer had it coming. Hence, natural disasters must be just punishments.

Holy Scripture contains examples of just this sort of thing. There are stories like the destruction of Sodom and Gomorrah, in which God destroyed a city for its wickedness (Genesis 19:24–25; 2 Peter

2:6). In contrast, some other stories flatly contradict this theology. Job, for instance, was just. The book that bears his name begins like this: "There was a man in the land of Uz whose name was Job, and that man was blameless and upright, one who feared God and turned away from evil" (Job 1:1). And yet, Job suffered. His misery had nothing to do with sin; on the contrary, he was a virtuous man. Job's story poses the question which philosophers and theologians have struggled with for centuries: How could a perfectly loving, omnipotent, and omniscient God allow good people to suffer? Presumably, a good and loving God would want to relieve suffering, not cause it. Likewise, an all-powerful and all-knowing God could prevent such suffering and would know how to do it. So how do we account for suffering like Job's?

To suggest that God offers compassion—that he suffers with us—is a start. But acknowledging God's empathy only goes so far. A sympathetic but ineffectual God is neither comforting nor true to biblical narrative. God has invited us to rely upon him. If we do not see him responding to our deepest distress, there is clearly something wrong with the picture.

Large, distant, natural disasters raise this question abstractly. Personal loss gets in your face. Among the many experiences of loss I have shared with people as a pastor, one stands out. When I was a seminarian spending a summer term as a hospital chaplain, I was once called into a birthing room. A baby had just died in childbirth. That was all I knew. An impossibly young woman was sitting up in bed, shell-shocked. Standing awkwardly next to her, a young man gazed blankly in her direction. Family members littered the room, contributing to an already thick silence. When I walked into the room, they looked up at me as if on cue. Every one of them looked sucker-punched. Their faces didn't betray grief or anger or even relief that somebody might break this unbearable silence with vaguely comforting words. Incomprehension was etched on every face.

This was years ago. My pastoral experience at that time could be reckoned in weeks. I would have remembered this scene just for its misery, but what happened next ensured that I could never forget it. I quietly expressed my sorrow for the family's loss and said prayers for the child and the family. Then another pastor arrived. This was the family's preacher. As a hospital chaplain, I greeted him and stepped aside so he could take his proper place with his people. In a jarringly upbeat tone, he told us all to remember that this was part of God's plan. It was God's will. God had a lesson for the young couple and for the whole family to learn. He instructed everybody to join hands and give thanks and glory to God.

My point here is not to criticize a fellow clergyperson. Stunned as I was, even then I knew he cared for this family. He believed what he said to them and thought it would bring comfort. Maybe you agree with him. I do not. Scripture reports again and again that God is deeply and intimately involved in even the smallest details of his creation, but that does not mean that earth will be like heaven. To put it a little differently, God's reign in heaven is perfect and complete. This is not so on earth—at least not yet. That is why Jesus himself taught us to pray, "Thy kingdom come, thy will be done, on earth as it is in heaven." God's reign on earth is a work in progress, and we have much to do to extend and reinforce that reign. Let me explain by looking with a little more care at what we mean when we say that God has a plan.

Plans, Blueprints, and Chessboards

For starters, it is probably best to be careful when we say that God has a plan. This phrase will suffice as shorthand in some situations, but remember that it is only a metaphor for the deeply mysterious way that God works his will for us. All metaphors have their limits. The concept of a "plan" might evoke the rigidity of a set of blueprints—a design that must be followed to the last small detail. Or, to some, God's plan might seem like a great chess master's strategy. God moves each of us according to his ultimate purpose. Whether we think in terms of blueprints or chessboards, God expresses his will coercively. He pushes things and people from behind, toward the position he wants them to occupy.

Set aside twenty-first-century sensibilities for a moment, and do not worry about how unacceptably cruel or manipulative Oprah would find such a God. Think instead of God's conversation with Abraham about the destruction of Sodom and Gomorrah (Genesis 18:22–33). Abraham bargained with God. "So, God, what if we found fifty righteous people? Would You spare the city then? How about forty? Thirty?" Or consider the story of the city of Nineveh's repentance. God sent Jonah to Nineveh by the less-than-scenic route, in the belly of a fish or whale, to tell the people there that God had had it with them; they were toast. When the Ninevites repented, God changed his mind and spared the city. Jonah pouted, but that is another story (Jonah 1:1–2; 17; 3:6–10; 4:1–2). Most importantly, remember the crucifixion. Jesus died on the cross for the very people who drove in the nails. he invites us to take up our crosses and follow him (Luke 23:34; Matthew 16:24).

Blueprints and chessboards do not convey the paradoxical richness of God's sovereignty and his vulnerability, his majesty and his humility, his unbending determination to keep his promises, and his responsiveness to soreheads and grumps like us. God is sovereign, yet we take part in connecting the dots of our lives. We can see this more clearly when we consider that God is teaching us how to be free.

Learning to Be Free

God does not push us around, and yet he rules the universe. God is reliable, but often things do not work out even when we are counting on God with all our heart. Preachers and theologians and philosophers have given us a huge range of sermons, essays, articles, and books to explain why bad things happen to good people and why some wicked people spend their whole lives laughing all the way to the bank.

Most of these preachers and authors try to reconcile God's goodness with people's suffering. Some say that God does not cause the suffering, or that he cannot prevent it. He is good, but not as powerful as advertised. He is really nice, but, maybe, not so reliable. Others say that the all-powerful God is justified in causing people suffering because they have it coming. God's got mojo, and he is good in a fierce, anxiety-inducing kind of way. He is so prickly that relying on him might make you feel a little too vulnerable.

Both of these theological strategies seem to be devoted to letting God off the hook for failing to make earth look like heaven. I am not interested in doing that. Nor are most of the people I know, when they are in the thick of what life throws at us.

When your child is sick, when your job is on the line, when your marriage is on the rocks, when your teenager is hooked on heroin, when your parent drifts in and out of the fog of Alzheimer's, and when the utility bill is due but your money is gone, you are more likely to cry out for help than to theorize about the nature of God.

When you are exhausted from chauffeuring your kids for the thousandth time, or sick of thinking you are too fat or too thin or too old, or so lonely in a crowded room that you find yourself fighting back tears, you are more likely to seek reassurance that living is worth all the sweat and tears than to worry about the logical consistency of your concept of God.

When you really want that promotion, when you want that project at work to be a homerun, when you want that college acceptance, when you want that girl to marry you, or that guy to marry somebody else, or just not to say the wrong thing on your first date, you will probably think about God being at your side rather than how his omnipotence squares with the tragedies of our world.

In other words, in your heart of hearts, you have one burning question: Can you rely on God? It is really not enough to merely know that he is watching and that he cares. I am not interested in being a character in one of God's soap operas. Can I count on him to come through for me? Yes, every time. Scripture tells us this, and I believe it to be true, but I did have to clear away some intellectual debris before it made sense. Perhaps you could use some conceptual decluttering yourself.

First of all, God's reign over natural things and processes is different from his reign among spiritual beings with minds, wills, and passions. Let me start with an example I recently heard from Timothy Keller to give you a sense of God's reign, its power, and its extent. The physical universe is so vast that we cannot comprehend it, so let us use a scale more suited to our finite minds. We know that the distance between the earth and the sun is ninety-two million miles. Picture, in your mind, this distance as the thickness of a single sheet of ordinary paper. To represent the distance between the earth and the next star in this scale, you would need a stack of papers seventy feet high. To depict the width of our galaxy, your stack of papers would have to be 310 miles high. Now hold on to your hat. There are between 100 and 200 billion galaxies in the universe. Our galaxy is just a speck of sand on the beach in comparison to the universe as a whole. Our stack of paper has just rocketed out of sight!

As we read in Colossians, "In him all things hold together" (Colossians 1:17). And how does he do it? Christ "upholds the universe by the *word of his power*" with the wave of a hand (Hebrews 1:3; italics mine). This is how God reigns over the physical universe. He sets planets in their orbits and sends electrons into quantum jumps by just saying so. But God's reign over the spiritual part of his kingdom looks very different, and understanding that difference will help us to understand why God's reign on earth can be thought of as a work in progress.

Molecules, planets and galaxies cannot know God. They are wonderfully made and they reflect his glory, but they cannot know him. They reflect God's will simply by doing what he says. They ask no questions because they cannot ask questions; they cannot say yes or no to God's direction. He speaks. They move. But in contrast, spiritual beings can say yes or no. God designed spiritual beings—angels, archangels, you, and me—so that we could know him. In fact, he created us to become who we are only when we come to know him. And knowing God is more than it sounds. To know God is to have a relationship with him on his terms, on the basis of who he really is.

Some people believe that life is about being comfortable. Others pursue success, pleasure, fame, or power with such tenacity that it must be their vision of the highest good. If they were right about that, then God really would have let a lot of us down. But they are not right. Human life is about much more than comfort, pleasure, applause, influence, or possessions.

God made us to love. I will discuss this in more detail in a later chapter. Love is a free gift, not an overwhelming passion. Created in God's image, we have the ability to choose a way to relate to God and to each other, regardless of how we happen to feel about God or the about other people at the moment. To love, we have to be free. But we must first learn to be free. This is where God is perfectly reliable. It might sound strange to say that we must learn to be free. We can make choices; aren't we already free?

If the height of freedom were willfulness, then this freedom thing would be a breeze. Just choose, and you are free. Jean-Paul Sartre said that we are condemned to be free; we cannot help ourselves. But that is not true. Drug addicts can tell you about how their once free choices led them into captivity. Their chose to begin using drugs, but eventually they lost the ability to choose to walk away from those drugs. Many addicts in recovery will tell you that grace saved them, although they may not use those exact words.

Freedom is learning how to choose. Two-year-olds, teenagers, and men in midlife can often be willful. A mature person knows how to be *willing*. Grownups do not need to have their own way. They know that Jesus Christ offers a more excellent one. To be free is to be willing, and we have to learn how to do this.

Look at the biblical record. By design, Adam was free. He could feed himself by plucking fruit from any tree in the garden of Eden—any tree. But just because you *can* do something does not mean that you *should*. God instructed Adam on how to exercise his freedom. Adam could pick fruit from any tree, but he should not pick from one of them. God told Adam to abstain from the fruit of the Tree of the Knowledge of Good and Evil (Genesis 2:15–17). In a sense, God said, "Here's a nice new will. Once you get the hang of it, you'll love it." The rest of the story, in which Adam and Eve ate the forbidden fruit and God expelled them from Eden, tells us one thing for sure: getting the hang of this freedom thing is easier said than done. The scriptural record underscores this point in different ways.

God promised a son to Abraham and Sarah. They waited a quarter of a century before God came through on his promise. (Abraham was a hundred years old, and Sarah ninety, but that is another story!) Then God commanded Abraham to sacrifice this son, Isaac (Genesis 22:1–14). Abraham needed to learn to choose for Isaac to be his son, not to be an idol to replace God. This is a lesson plenty of us could also stand to learn. Our children would appreciate it; they are not here to justify our existences.

In another example, after the Hebrews passed through the Red Sea, they wandered in the desert for forty years before reaching the Promised Land. Geographically speaking, their trip should have been a three-week walk. God himself led them through the desert as a pillar of cloud by day and a pillar of fire by night. So why did he take the scenic route? During their time in the desert, the Hebrews were learning how to be free, and how to live freely in covenant with God (Exodus 19:4–6).

The Sinaitic Covenant was the agreement between God and the people; it was the law. I have resisted using the word "obedience" up to this point because of its negative connotation to contemporary ears.

Many consider obedience to be the opposite of freedom, but nothing could be further from the truth. In his law, God does not impose a capricious set of demands upon us. The purpose of his law is to guide us to learn how to love. The law, which Jesus himself uttered, boils down to loving God in your very marrow and loving your neighbor as you love yourself. God does not want us to slavishly follow rules for fear of punishment or in hopes of personal advancement. He wants us to learn to be free and willing. I will explain this further.

Willfulness is a part of us all. We define freedom as pursuing our own desires. Sometimes our desires and God's law run in conflicting directions. As long as we think of freedom as doing what we want to do, we will sometimes see obedience as God overriding our will. In this perspective, obedience requires forsaking freedom. But there is another way to understand free will. We can exercise our will by choosing to align our will with God's. In other words, we can be willing instead of willful. This can certainly be a struggle, but it is a struggle between our own desires. We exert our will to choose the higher good commanded by God over a lesser good we desire.

Only one of us has ever gotten this willingness business right: Jesus. He did so for all of us. Do not for a moment think it was as easy as falling off a log. Look at Jesus in the garden of Gethsemane: "'Father, if you are willing, remove this cup from me; yet, not my will but yours be done.' Then an angel from heaven appeared to him and gave him strength. In his anguish he prayed more earnestly, and his sweat became like great drops of blood falling down on the ground" (Luke 22:42–44). Jesus was willing. He came through for us, once and for all. He died for all the sins we have committed with our willful hearts.

He is still willing. He and the Father send the Holy Spirit to those of us who accept the lordship of Jesus Christ, and the Holy Spirit changes our hearts. Your will follows your heart, but the Holy Spirit's work involves stretching and even breaking your heart.

Does God Plan to Break Your Heart?

God runs a tight ship. That is what the opening scenes of the film *The Adjustment Bureau* suggest. We never get to see God, or the Chairman, as he is called in the movie, but we do get to watch his angels at work.

Dressed in sixties-era suits, they busy themselves with keeping God's plan on track. They make minor adjustments in our lives when chance or a wayward choice threatens to send God's unbelievably intricate plan off the rails. These midlevel angelic executives do not use major catastrophes or eye-popping miracles to steer events along the divine path. Rather, they make small adjustments that effect cosmic ripples. Spilled cups of coffee and dropped cell-phone calls serve to nudge events back on track.

The plot centers on a love story. David Norris (played by Matt Damon) and Elise Sellas (played by Emily Blunt) are irresistibly drawn to each other, but unfortunately for them, their relationship is not part of God's plan. The action that unfolds pits the lovers' freedom to choose to spend their lives together against God's plan and his influence in keeping them apart. If you want to know how it turns out, see the movie—no spoilers here. But the question posed by the film is one for those of us who are looking to rely on God in our daily lives to consider carefully: Does God plan to break your heart?

In the preceding pages I have already stated that God connects the dots for his creation as a whole, and for each of us as individuals. He has a dream or a vision of how it all fits together. Metaphors of blueprints and chessboards cannot account for our freedom to choose, or for the responsibility we bear for our actions. However, the premise of *The Adjustment Bureau* resonates with the biblical message that we are each learning to be free. God created us to love him and to love our neighbors. Without freedom, we could not give our love as a gift. We have a spiritual learning curve ahead of us, and it involves wrenching our hearts.

So, does God plan to break your heart? Does God's design involve suffering and sorrow? Yes and no. The answer depends on what we are really asking here. So let's ask some different versions of that question.

Does God press buttons to create earthquakes, volcanos, or tsunamis in order to punish us or to teach us lessons? He could, but I suspect that he doesn't. Our freedom requires an orderly, predictable universe. If we could not foresee the consequences of our actions with a degree of confidence, then freedom would not have much meaning. Imagine a world in which jumping off a roof might cause you to break your ankle one time, but another time, it might teleport you to Mars;

the same roof and the same leap would yield wildly different results. In a world such as this, I could always say, "It is not my fault." I might even begin to wonder what difference at all my choices and actions made. However, natural law gives us a world in which we can make choices reasonably, and hold each other accountable for what we do and what we leave undone. Sometimes, suffering results from natural processes. Why doesn't God just suspend the law of nature? Well, if God made a habit of suspending natural law every time suffering, disappointment, or sorrow resulted from it, then there would simply not be a natural law.

That is not to say that God's governance of the natural universe is limited solely to his authorship of natural law. This point is one of the intriguing themes explored in *The Adjustment Bureau*. God nudges things in a way that does not tear the fabric of his creation. The Bible depicts many miraculous interventions which occur in the ordinary course of events. God stops the sun in the sky and he parts the Red Sea (Joshua 10:13; Exodus 13:21–22). Jesus raises the dead, heals lepers with a word and a touch, restores sight to the blind, and walks on water (see Matthew 9:18; 19; 23–25; Luke 7:11–15; John 11:38–44; Matthew 8:2–3; Mark 8:22–26; John 9:1–20; Mark 6:45–52).

But miracles are, by necessity, rare exceptions to the general rule of order. Nudging—well, that is a different matter. We are affected by God's nudges, along with the many other influences in our lives. Sometimes he allows us to suffer pain or sorrow in order to help us avoid calamity in the future. You might unaccountably feel like picking up the phone and calling an old friend, only to discover that he has recently received a dire diagnosis. Somebody might say something that helps you see the solution to your marital problem, even though she is talking about something completely different. How could she know that the ingredients of a recipe would remind you why you really love your spouse? God does not nudge us toward suffering and sorrow. He nudges us toward reconciliation, mercy, joy, patience, peace, and justice. In this sense, we can say that God does not plan to break your heart.

Now let's ask the question in a different way. Can we really be what God dreams we can if our hearts are never broken? This framing uncovers one of our basic misconceptions. Suffering, sickness, disappointment, and the like seem unfair to us, as though God created us to be comfortable and entertained. Any departure from this program feels uncaring, even cruel. Of course, comfort and entertainment have their place. However, they are not the highest good for us to achieve. Instead, love occupies that place. Love grows and matures us by stretching and even breaking our hearts.

C. S. Lewis summed it up brilliantly in this oft-quoted passage from *The Four Loves*: "To love at all is to be vulnerable. Love anything, and your heart will certainly be wrung and possibly broken. If you want to make sure of keeping it intact, you must give your heart to no one, not even to an animal. Wrap it carefully round with hobbies and little luxuries; avoid all entanglements; lock it up safe in the casket or coffin of your selfishness. But in that casket—safe, dark, motionless, airless—it will change. It will not be broken; it will become unbreakable, impenetrable, irredeemable."

You can feel your heart pulling apart when your child's favorite toy breaks, when your friend loses her husband, when your mother cannot remember how to find her way home. When you say goodbye to a beloved pet, leave your hometown for the last time, or send your daughter off to college, your heart stretches and tears a bit. That is what love is. Heartbreak of this sort makes us more, not less. And God does not merely observe our heartbreak from a distance, giving us the medicine that he knows is good for us. He is right there, in the midst of it, with us. The cross represents God's heart, broken for us. The empty tomb and the risen Christ teach us that our broken hearts, in God's hands, lead to love and life eternal.

God plans to break our hearts. Not to cause meaningless suffering or to mar what would otherwise be wonderful lives; God loves us enough to share with us his own capacity to love. Paradoxically, breaking our hearts heals our hearts. God does more than nurture immature hearts so they will grow. The fall disfigured our hearts, so without God's intervention, we will always love in distorted ways. God gives us new hearts (Ezekiel 36:22–32). God makes us a new creation as a part of his larger work of reclaiming the creation as his own. The Sovereign Lord promises that one day, his reign will be as complete and perfect on earth as it is in heaven. This is the topic to which we will turn next.

A New Heaven and A New Earth

Jesus knew how to stay on message. Here is the sound bite: "The time is fulfilled, and the kingdom of God has come near; repent, and believe in the good news" (Mark 1:15). His parables and sermons convey what the kingdom of God is like. But Jesus was not interested in telling us about some distant place to which we might someday escape. That is why he refused to rely on words alone to get his point across. Jesus healed the sick, cast out demons, walked on water, calmed storms, died on a cross, and rose from the dead. The good news is that God is reasserting his authority in this messy world we inhabit. He is doing it through his Son, Jesus Christ. What sort of authority is God reasserting? Why would a sovereign God *need* to reassert anything? Let's tackle these questions one at a time.

The scope of God's authority is infinite. He sees the big picture and concerns himself with even the smallest detail. "The Lord has established his throne in the heavens, and his kingdom rules over all" (Psalm 103:19). God reigns as a good king over his kingdom. He is neither a chess master nor a passive spectator. While he may at times be content to work through the minor nudges of his angels, as depicted in the film *The Adjustment Bureau*, in the end, he insists on being the hands-on King of his entire kingdom, both of heaven and of earth.

His reign on earth was perfect in the garden of Eden. Adam and Eve were unselfconsciously naked (Genesis 3:8–11). They did not have to keep secrets, or put their best foot forward, or draw defensive boundaries, or pretend to be something they were not. They were at peace with each other, with themselves, and with the world they inhabited. Their lives were full of purpose and rich with meaning. God gave them the desire to make a contribution, and he gave them a context within which that was possible. God made Adam his gardener and put him in a garden suited to his skills and temperament (Genesis 2:15).

God gave Adam and Eve the gift of freedom so that they could love him, tend his garden, and share with each other respect, compassion, and a common purpose. For them, freedom never meant just doing whatever they felt like doing. God set parameters for exercising freedom: "And the Lord God commanded the man, saying, 'You may surely eat of every tree of the garden, but of the tree of the knowledge of good and evil you shall not eat, for in the day that you eat of it you shall surely die'" (Genesis 2:16–17). God set this limitation because the purpose of freedom is to glorify God by nurturing and increasing the good that he gives us to tend in the first place.

Adam and Eve were free to choose to follow the path of love and nurturing, or to go another way. But here is a key point: freedom allows us to choose which path to take. Our free will cannot change the final destinations of the various paths before us. God showed Adam and Eve the way of nurturing, love, and growth, but they chose a different way, which led to fruitless toil, suffering, and decay. To put it simply, eating of the Tree of Knowledge of Good and Evil amounted to taking the path of death (Genesis 3:16–24).

Their choice to eat the forbidden fruit expressed an enduring spiritual posturing: "I can find my own way. I do not need to rely upon God to make my life meaningful and valuable. My achievements and my possessions and my social standing make me significant. My cunning and my strength will keep me safe and secure." In other words, "I will connect the dots of my life. After all, my life is my own." From that point on, Adam, Eve, and all the rest of us shifted our focus. Instead of focusing on God, we became absorbed in grasping and forging and asserting our own significance. We strain to justify our own existences, and as a result, we increasingly focus on ourselves.

It seemed like a good idea at the time. Each person could be free to pursue his or her own version of happiness. As the story in Genesis goes, Satan lured Adam and Eve onto this path. He said he was doing them a favor, helping them to express their innermost selves. The film *The Devil's Advocate* paints a disturbingly convincing portrait of the Tempter. At one point, Satan (played by Al Pacino) says, "I'm a fan of man!" God, in contrast, is always holding out on us. It was and still is a seductive, highly effective lie.

The bitter irony is that as long as our own earthly happiness is our chief delight, we will never find it. We will simply grow more and more self-absorbed, and our self-absorption undermines the very actions that can give us happiness: loving God because he is God, and loving others because they are his children. If we make delighting in God and loving our neighbors our highest priority, happiness will result. On the other hand, if we pursue happiness above all else, it will continually slip from our grasp. In the next chapter, we will examine this point in detail. As a result of the fall, the human heart is turned away from God. "The intention of man's heart is evil from his youth" (Genesis 8:21).

God's response is to redeem his creation. It is important to recognize that the fall erased not only the inclination of the human heart, but also the lines connecting the dots of the whole of creation. Consider, for example, the state of the natural world even after Noah and his family emerged from the ark. In the garden of Eden, animals did not prey on one another. The wolf could lie down with the lamb and the lamb did not need antianxiety medication. In contrast, in the post-flood world, animals struggled to survive precisely because they devoured one another. God told Noah, "The fear of you and the dread of you shall be upon every beast of the earth and upon every bird of the heavens, upon everything that creeps on the ground and all the fish of the sea. Into your hand they are delivered. Every moving thing that lives shall be food for you. And as I gave you the green plants, I give you everything" (Genesis 9:2–3).

God is not content to remove humans from his creation and consign the rest of it to destruction. He will renew the earth. He begins by renewing the human heart. "And I will give you a new heart, and a new spirit I will put within you. And I will remove the heart of stone from your flesh and give you a heart of flesh" (Ezekiel 36:26). He does so even before his redeeming work for the whole of creation is complete. In other words, followers of Christ dwell as hope-inspired creatures in the midst of a still-fallen earth. But God's plan is not to teleport us away. Instead, he promises to renew the whole creation.

The apostle Paul taught about a future glory: "For the creation waits with eager longing for the revealing of the sons of God. For the creation was subjected to futility, not willingly, but because of him who subjected it, in hope that the creation itself will be set free from its bondage to corruption and obtain the freedom of the glory of the children of God" (Romans 8:19–21). The whole creation was subjected to the disfigurement of the fall. God will restore it to its goodness and beauty.

St. John makes the point even more boldly. In the second coming of the crucified and risen Jesus Christ, God will make a new heaven and a new earth. God promises to renew this earth on which we dwell. He will not pluck us up and away from this place, but instead, will restore our earthly dwelling place to its proper glory, and dwell here with us. The New Jerusalem descends from heaven to earth:

> Then I saw a new heaven and a new earth, for the first heaven and the first earth had passed away, and the sea was no more. And I saw the holy city, new Jerusalem, coming down out of heaven from God, prepared as a bride adorned for her husband. And I heard a loud voice from the throne saying, "Behold, the dwelling place of God is with man. He will dwell with them, and they will be his people, and God himself will be with them as their God. He will wipe away every tear from their eyes, and death shall be no more, neither shall there be mourning, nor crying, nor pain anymore, for the former things have passed away."
> —Revelation 21:1–4

In other words, God promises to connect the dots. Trusting in God's promise, trusting his sovereign will, makes it possible for us to live in hope. By placing faith in the promises of Jesus Christ, his followers dwell on this earth as the very place that God will redeem and dwell in. It is not our role to make this earth into his dwelling place. We lack the power to redeem the creation. Instead, motivated by the vision of a new heaven and a new earth, and empowered by our trust in God's sovereignty, we followers of Jesus can apply the laws of the new heaven and the new earth in our lives, on the earth we know. God works through us on our best days to heal something broken, or to make something disfigured whole again, to connect the dots. This life unfolds after the fall in anticipation of the new heaven and the new earth. Can we have happiness in the meantime? What would it look like? That is the topic of the next chapter.

CHAPTER TWO

FINDING HAPPINESS

If you ask people on the street what they want out of life, you will likely hear many of them say, "I just want to be happy." With a little digging, you could get them to elaborate on what would make them happy: a rewarding job, career advancement, a loving spouse, healthy and successful children, a nice home, and good health. The specifics of an individual's list will vary, but most will have something in common: the items on the list will be external circumstances. People everywhere pursue happiness. They look for something that will connect the dots of their lives. Very often, people assume that the inner conditions associated with happiness—contentment, tranquility, and joy—result from achieving some specific set of external circumstances.

Let me be very clear. Our desire for rewarding work, happy marriages, thriving children, and comfortable homes can be very good for us. Wanting such things is part of being human. God designed us to enjoy these earthly things, and he wants to provide them. The Bible offers instruction about how to flourish in this life. Wisdom guides us in marriage, parenting, friendship, and work. (For passages on marriage see Proverbs 5:1–18; 31:10, Ephesians 5:22–33; for parenting see Deuteronomy 4:9, Proverbs 17:6, 22:6, and 23:13, and Ephesians 6:1–4; for friendship see Proverbs 17:17, 18:24, 27:6, 27:10, 27:17, John 15:13, and James 4:4; and for passages on work see Exodus 23:12, Psalm 104:23 and 128:2, Proverbs 12:14, 14:23, Ecclesiastes 5:8–20, and Ephesians 4:28).

But even if you achieve all of these things so that to an outside observer, your life appears full to bursting, you could still be plagued by the sense of something missing. You may have all the pieces, but they do not fit together to make you feel whole; the dots of your life do not connect. You may believe that some earthly achievement or set of circumstances will connect the dots for you. But those successes, awards, and material comforts will always let you down if you ask them to make your life truly significant. Only God can do that. And so, the starting place for a meaningful, significant life is the starting place of wisdom: fear of the Lord (Proverb 9:10).

It is part of God's design for us to want earthly things. Life begins to come apart when we assume that our happiness hinges on our external circumstances. If we were to define God making us happy as his providing us with the external conditions to give us our desired internal life, then we would have to conclude that God is not devoted to human happiness. In any case, God does not define happiness in this way.

God intends to give us a spiritual life in which our peace, joy, integrity, and power are so great that they not only endure any set of material conditions but also transform those external circumstances. In other words, God promises to connect the dots of our lives. His aim is not to make us indifferent to our surroundings, nor to make us live with just the promise of escaping them. God promises to connect the dots of our lives so that we can do earthly good in the face of adversity, setbacks, long odds, and heartaches. To be genuinely happy on this earth, we have to be clear about the source of happiness. Expecting our outer circumstances to make us happy turns things upside down—or, more precisely, inside out.

Inside and Out

This brief passage from Proverbs helps us to see how God intends our inner lives to define and even transform our outer lives: "A man's spirit sustains him in sickness, but a crushed spirit who can bear?" (Proverb 18:14 NIV) Your spirit can sustain you, even in spite of physical illness. We probably all know and admire someone who suffers from chronic pain or struggles with severe disabilities, yet keeps a positive attitude, who continues to make a contribution in the lives of others, and seems never to feel resentful or defeated. Conversely, people who are the picture of health, at the top their career ladders, married to spouses who turn everyone's heads, and parents to *summa cum laude* students could be crying in misery on the inside.

Because we Westerners are so achievement-oriented, we are very likely to come away with from this with the wrong lesson. Too many of us are quick to hear the false gospel of attitude adjustment; we have a misconception that happiness boils down to choosing to accept and love ourselves just the way we are. So, we indulge in various techniques for fostering positive self-image. For instance, some "experts" focus on the importance of self-esteem by teaching techniques to produce positive self-thoughts, or to applaud yourself for your own efforts.

While it is important to acknowledge our strengths and successes, and to accept and to learn from our missteps, in no way does the Gospel suggest that we can rely upon only ourselves for happiness. Let me counter this misconception with words from the apostle Paul: "The fruit of the Spirit is love, joy, peace, patience, kindness, goodness, faithfulness, gentleness, self-control" (Galatians 5:22–23). In other words, we do not gain the inner conditions by which we define happiness as a result of our own efforts. Rather, when we rely upon Christ, the Holy Spirit produces a fruit within us—it is not derived from any external circumstance.

Even given this truth, that the Holy Spirit molds the inner lives of his believers, we must not leap to the wrong conclusion. Belief in God will not make us perpetually cheerful, nor shield us from the changes and chances of this world. Jesus is the very best example of that. He wept at Lazarus's tomb. He felt grief at his friend's death, and compassion for Martha and Mary as they mourned the loss of their brother (John 11:32–35). Jesus teaches us by example that there is nothing faithless or unchristian about sorrow. Here are some more examples that may reflect your own experiences.

When my children or my wife are sick or sad, I become concerned and troubled for them. I have comforted people on the deaths of sons and daughters. My heart felt very heavy to see them so distraught. One friend of mine was denied tenure at a university. He was disappointed and concerned about the next steps of his career. Another friend proposed to a beautiful young woman and was rejected, making him stunned and confused. Arduous external circumstances and rocky emotions are part of earthly life. If we pin our hopes for happiness on earthly things, then when we suffer, we may falsely conclude that God does not love us, or that we are failures. A striking number of very faithful people have confided in me their belief that the difficult passages of their life were caused by bad things they had done or by their inability to pray in the right way. Without meaning to, they gave fleeting temporal circumstances the power to shape the meaning of their lives. They unwittingly expected earth to be heaven, and when it was not, they decided that they themselves were somehow to blame.

If, instead, we remember that *God* is connecting the dots, we can begin to receive the gift of hope. Times of trial and adversity can paradoxically become occasions for hope-inspired motivation. Hope leads us through challenges and trying emotions to anticipate what God will do next, and to remember that he is working for our personal good and for the greater good. For instance, if we feel genuine compassion for the sick and the sorrowful, then we are wounded right along with the ones who suffer. Jesus himself said, "If anyone would come after me, let him deny himself and take up his cross and follow me" (Mark 8:34). If you think that God's greatest blessings are the comforts, status, and rewards of this world, then Jesus' words do not make sense. But if you are shaped by hope, you can see that God wants more for us. As Paul said, "Bear one another's burdens, and so fulfill the law of Christ" (Galatians 6:2). Love that costs nothing leaves our hearts unchanged. Bearing the burdens of others expands our hearts and makes us more, not less, capable of loving. Hearts stretched by compassion and mercy grow in their capacity to love, because Jesus himself initiates that kind of love in his followers to make us more than we could make ourselves to be. Paul put it this way: "Therefore, if anyone is in Christ, he is a new creation. The old has passed away; behold, the new has come" (2 Corinthians 5:17).

Career failure and romantic rejection are not happy experiences for anyone, and yet, they can be precisely the means through which God does more for us than we could ourselves imagine. Some are tempted to justify their own existences through career achievements, or to seek their worth from the love they receive from a man or woman. But no finite achievement or person can satisfy our infinite desire for significance. Solomon reflected on the folly of following that path:

"Vanity of vanities . . . All is vanity" (Ecclesiastes 1:2). A career failure or a romantic heartbreak can be God's way of turning us away from the empty pursuit of an idol that will never deliver what it promises.

God wants more for us than mere contentment with external circumstances. He wants us to enjoy a seamless relationship with him and unbroken fellowship with his other children. He accomplishes this for us in the cross of Christ. God changes us, in Christ, so that we can see our Redeemer face to face, and sit joyfully at the great banquet feast with all of Christ's honored guests in the new heaven and the new earth.

Please do not assume now that we should reject the pleasures of this life. God has placed us in a wonderful world filled with good things; food and drink, significant work, close friends, the love of family, and the beauty of nature are gifts from God. He gives them to us so that we can be happy. He is a God of blessing, and happiness is one of his blessings. But neither our material circumstances nor our fleeting emotions is God's highest blessing for us. In fact, if we confuse our earthly contentment with God's greatest blessing, we are losing sight of his chief desire for us. God does not want our earthly contentment to stand in the way of our eternal life in his Kingdom. Eternal life is not merely an earthly existence that goes on forever; it is a different kind of life. We begin to glimpse it here in space and time, to get a hint of it, and even yearn for it, when we refuse to let pursuit of the good things of this world assume an improper place in our lives.

To make a clearer distinction between finite contentment and eternal happiness, we must look at desire. God equipped us with the capacity for desire. Just as our physical survival requires food and shelter, our souls yearn for companionship and a sense of significance. Above all, we desire fellowship with God. It is common to talk about the pursuit of happiness as the search for our heart's desires. But the matter is more complicated than that. Our desires can conflict with each other. We can desire harmful things, and we can also be mistaken about what will satisfy our desires. Sometimes, our desires commandeer our souls and rule them like tyrants.

Let me put it this way: desire is the third rail of the soul. On subways tracks, the third rail provides electricity to power the train. The high energy carried by the third rail far exceeds a household current; touching the rail results in electrocution. In this analogy, desire provides energy for our vitality or fuel for our destruction. Without desire, without energy propelling us toward a destination, we are lifeless. And yet, desire is dangerous. We can and sometimes do yearn for things that could lead us to spiritual destruction.

All desire is about wanting more. When we get the idea of "more" right, when we put proper limits on desire, then life is sweet, joyful, tranquil, and contented. When we get it wrong, we get spiritual electrocution. Let's look first at keeping desire within its proper bounds. Jesus teaches his disciples that earthly desires are good when they serve the purposes of heaven. He makes this point clearly when he teaches his disciples what we today call The Lord's Prayer.

Daily Bread for an Eternal Kingdom

If you struggle with saying "when," do not expect your desires to be any help to you. That is not their job. Desire is all about "more"—it's why we end up regretting that second piece of pecan pie at Thanksgiving. Do not blame your desires when you find yourself wanting something that you know is bad for you; their job is to want more. Assessing health, quality, or helpfulness is above their pay grade. We see the nature of desire in simple, everyday experiences. Think about all the times you stand at the open refrigerator scanning its contents for something to eat. You do not know what you want; you just want something. And after devouring several different things, you realize you did not want any of it. You are not satisfied. You want more.

The Greek philosopher Plato argued that reason is the natural master of desire. Reason instructs desire about proper objects, and reins in desire by instructing the will to clamp down when desire's proper limits are met. At least, that is what happens in a perfectly ordered soul. Christian Reformers like Martin Luther held that that there are no perfectly ordered souls. In fact, we are all upside down. We want what we want. Often we want the wrong thing or too much of a good thing. Desire compels the will to action, and after we have acted, reason conjures up a rationalization to get us off the hook.

Only following Christ will turn us right side up—but not because he has new techniques for controlling desire, or because he supercharges our wills, or even because he extinguishes our errant passions. Jesus teaches us how to get "more" right. In The Sermon on the Mount (Matthew 5–7), Jesus has plenty to say about desire. Warning us about its destructive power, Jesus tells us that it is better to gouge out an eye or to hack off a hand than to let them become the instruments of sinful desire (Matthew 5:29–30). Now that he has our attention, he teaches us how to pray what we now routinely call the Lord's Prayer, a simple but powerful teaching about desire which can be easy to miss. It is important for us to see the Lord's Prayer as more than just a set of words. It models a way of life, a hope-shaped life, and it helps us to see how our earthly desires fit into the greater context of our relationship with God. It teaches us about genuine happiness.

The prayer begins like this: "Our Father in heaven, hallowed be your name" (Matthew 6:9). Jesus teaches us that we secure the external circumstances that satisfy our desires in the broader context of acknowledging God as God: by praising him and glorifying him for his godliness. He is the treasure we seek above all others, and nothing nor no one can compare with him. Before we ask for daily bread, Jesus reminds us that we need daily bread in order to glorify God's name by dedicating our lives to his kingdom. "Your kingdom come, your will be done, on earth as it is in heaven" (Matthew 6:10). God nourishes and shelters our bodies so we can give them to him as a living sacrifice (Romans 12:1).

Desire itself would just skip right to the middle of the prayer: "Give us this day our daily bread" (Matthew 6:11). But if we were to reduce happiness to acquiring the external circumstances to satisfy our desires, then in essence, we would be rewriting the Lord's Prayer by placing this phrase at the very beginning. More precisely, we would be boiling down the whole prayer to the two-word phrase, "Give us"—or, to be honest, "Give me"—fixing on our personal feelings of satisfaction and viewing God as merely a means to our earthly contentment. In focusing on our personal comfort and contentment, we would be forgetting about the Kingdom of God, and about our hope for the new heaven and the new earth.

But in contrast, when we assume the hopeful posture taught at the beginning of the prayer, our petition to God to "give us" is something else entirely; it acknowledges our utter dependence upon him. This is the only posture that allows us to see God as the generous provider who never holds out on us. It frees us from the anxious belief that we have to grab and grasp for ourselves, or else go wanting.

Concentrating on "this day" is easier said than done, but this is Jesus' next instruction about desire. We are often inclined to race ahead in our imaginations. Even when we have enough for today, we worry about having enough tomorrow, or next week, or next year. Jesus is not suggesting that we live *for* today, or that we toss aside planning and preparation. He clearly tells us to live *in* today. If we race ahead in time with our imaginations, we turn the "more" engine into overdrive, and become dissatisfied with what God has provided us on this day. Jesus amplifies this point further in his sermon. "Therefore do not worry about tomorrow, for tomorrow will worry about itself. Each day has enough trouble of its own" (Matthew 6:34).

Finally, Jesus teaches us to ask for our "daily bread." We must learn to be genuinely content with what we have today instead of focusing on the "more" that others have, or that we might get tomorrow. That we can want things we do not need is not a news flash to anyone. But Jesus' point goes deeper than that. God's daily bread is often far more than we need, or far more than we even imagined (Ephesians 3:20). Taking the wrong attitude toward what we have right now can deprive us of the joy and peace that God intended for us when he gave it to us in the first place.

We might want more bread, or a different kind of bread, or something else in addition to bread, but regardless, when our desires are functioning normally, we will experience at least a fleeting sense of satisfaction when we get what we want. When our desires are fulfilled, our grumbling and ingratitude might diminish the joy that God wants for us, but we will have a sense of satiety before we lose sight of it. However, desire itself can go terribly wrong. In an apparently paradoxical way, getting what we want can lead to greater and even more painful yearning, rather than satisfaction.

Cravings

Enough is enough—except when it is not. We can want more even when we have enough. This is one way that desire leads us down the rabbit hole. We have all wanted the occasional second piece of cake or extra helping of meatloaf. It can, of course, be a challenge to acknowledge the healthy limits of food and drink (and exercise and work and episodes of *I Love Lucy*). However, there is another dysfunction of desire that is not about a mere failure to exercise moderation or to consume proper portions. Sometimes, desire is a form of insanity in which "more" becomes your life's purpose: you want more precisely because you are getting what you want. In other words, getting the very thing you have been chasing can compel you to want it all the more desperately.

Addictions are a clear example of what I am talking about. Recovering alcoholics avoid "the first drink" like the plague. The first drink does not quench an alcoholic's thirst; it creates a desire for the next drink. And the next one. And the next. If you don't have experience with addiction, this may not seem relevant to you. But have you ever wanted a larger salary? A bigger house? The latest car, or iPad, or laptop? Many of us earn a salary that covers all of our needs as well as some luxuries. My house is so big I have a room just for my car (it's called a carport), and some of us have an extra room just in case someone might show up and want to use it. I have a ton of friends whose second-generation iPads now seem to them like papyrus and ink because the iPad 3 has just come out.

We all know what it is like to want more precisely when we have enough, or maybe even more than enough. In the Bible, this feeling is sometimes translated as craving. Craving is exactly what beset the Hebrews as they wandered in the desert between escaping through the Red Sea and finally arriving in the Promised Land. The Psalmist puts it bluntly: "But they did not stop their craving, though the food was still in their mouths" (Psalm 78:30 BCP). The Hebrews had been slaves in Egypt. Nothing in their past had prepared them to survive in the desert; they were utterly dependent upon God for sustenance. He gave them manna to eat each morning. Their job was simply to collect enough to feed them for the day, and to trust that more manna would appear the following morning. With the exception of manna collected in preparation for Sabbath rest, any manna collected in excess of daily needs would spoil by the next morning (Exodus 16:2–20). God was teaching the Hebrews a healthy spiritual posture, to rely upon God's provision today and trust in God's provision for tomorrow. Peace and justice will follow. The alternative is to grab what you want assuming you will not get enough otherwise. It may seem sensible and realistic to take care of yourself first in an environment of potential scarcity, but ultimately, it leads to misery.

Once we abandon our faith in God's reliability, we focus increasingly on the fact that we could always have more: more money for retirement, more recognition at work, a higher GPA at school, another pair of shoes, or piece of jewelry. Yesterday's applause fades so quickly that before the curtain has even closed, we begin to want the next standing ovation and to worry that we will never again be on stage—whatever stage that may be. As Solomon put it, "He who loves money will not be satisfied with money, nor he who loves wealth with his income; this also is vanity" (Ecclesiastes 5:10).

Craving is anxious awareness that the satisfaction of the moment is fleeting, mingled with fear of being left unsatisfied in the future. It makes us scramble to get more; contentment has left the building. Paradoxically, we do not derive contentment from knowing when enough is enough. We actually experience contentment by recognizing that we are creatures in deep need. We need God's love, his forgiveness, his mercy, and his provision. Contentment comes into full bloom when we see that we have all of these things. As Peter says, "Blessed be the God and Father of our Lord Jesus Christ! According to his great mercy, he has caused us to be born again to a living hope through the resurrection of Jesus Christ from the dead, to an inheritance that is imperishable, undefiled, and unfading, kept in heaven for you" (1 Peter 1:3–4).

God already offers what we most deeply desire. He offers us himself in his Son, Jesus Christ. The cross is an enduring sign of God's self-offering to us, even while we were rejecting him (Romans 5:8). We have only to receive our desire by faith; the only thing standing in our way is us. As long as we grasp and grab for ourselves what we want, we can never receive it freely. And in fact, the very thing we most want can only be given as a gift.

The soul can be corroded from within by wanting too much of a good thing, or simply never being satisfied with enough. Desire can be more destructive and dangerous. We can be drawn to things that are at once toxic for us and lethal for those around us. We can and sometimes do desire harmful things under the mistaken impression that they will be our soul's delight when we finally lay our hands on them.

Bait and Switch

I learned an enduring lesson about desire when I was five years old. Every morning at breakfast, I would stare at the back of the cereal box, at the picture of a WWI biplane sweeping through the air. The pilot's scarf was streaming behind him. The plane's guns were blazing. For only three box tops, a genuine replica of a WWI warplane could be mine. My five-year-old heart was set. I doggedly worked my way through three boxes of cereal that I absolutely hated and no one else would touch. (Well, strictly speaking, I also poured out several bowls of cereal when nobody was looking.) My desire to have that plane drove me relentlessly. I daydreamed endlessly about being that pilot. I could see myself bursting through the clouds, descending furiously on a numerically superior foe, and narrowly winning harrowing dogfights with superior skill and courage. Finally, I collected the required box tops and mailed them off to the cereal company. After what seemed like decades, the package arrived. Inside was a gray plastic plane with a wingspan of two inches, at most. It was not at all what I had had in mind.

My childhood disappointment over that plane is a tame example of a spiritual bait and switch: idolatry. It looks something like this. Our desires fall for a sort of false advertising, and then we find ourselves organizing our lives around the pursuit of this thing that promises to make us happy. Eventually, we discover that we have been taken in by a false promise, and find ourselves emptier than when we first began.

In the classic bait-and-switch scheme, a retailer advertises a product at a low price in order to get customers into the store. However, when customers arrive, they learn that the sale item is out of stock, and sales clerks then pressure them to buy a different, in-stock product of higher quality than the advertised one. It is, of course, more expensive. This sales tactic works by making something appear far more desirable than it really is. What we want is attainable, but not right away. It is just out of reach for a brief season. To get the thing we want, we have to give up many other things. In fact, the deadliest spiritual bait and switch makes us devote ourselves entirely to the thing we pursue. We become idol worshippers.

The Bible teaches us this principle through vivid stories. Adam and Eve, for instance, ate the forbidden fruit in Eden. They believed that it held the secrets to moral wisdom and godly existence. In reality, eating the fruit introduced them to shame, fear, conflict, alienation, and death (Genesis 3:5; 10). Another example is when Moses ascended Mount Sinai to receive the Ten Commandments. He took much longer to return than the Hebrews expected, so they tossed aside not only Moses but also God himself, and fashioned a golden calf to worship instead. They believed that they had erected a comfortable god, one that could never leave them, nor ever lead them to unfamiliar, frightening places. In fact, they placed all their hopes on an inanimate object that was powerless to love them, protect them, guide them, or sustain them (Exodus 32:1–14).

Desire can focus our lives. In his Sermon on the Mount, Jesus said, "Blessed are the pure in heart" (Matthew 5:8). Philosopher Soren Kierkegaard said that being pure of heart means being able to desire one thing above all others, that is, having all other desires fall into line behind the central desire. We put on hold or completely disregard the desires which we decide are inferior. We may sacrifice our relationships, our health, our financial security, or our reputations for the sake of the overriding desire.

God designed our hearts to desire above all others one thing: a relationship with him. When we pursue righteousness, everything else will follow. Jesus said, "But seek first his kingdom and his righteousness, and all these things will be given to you as well" (Matthew 6:33). God is not one thing among other things. He is the source and the sustainer of all things.

Our desire for him is not like any other desire. Our desire for him organizes all other desires, and it focuses our thoughts and our will. It is our desire to base our lives on something important, to cling to something that justifies our existence. The problem is that we humans can focus our desire on objects that have no chance of satisfying us. Idolatry is the desire to make anything other than God the god of our lives. Sex, money, power, career success, and fame are among the common idols people worship. In their proper place, these things can help to make our lives rich and rewarding. They promise us happiness, but in the end, they cannot defeat death, overcome tragedy, or redeem failure. When we dedicate our lives to these common idols, in return they give us only emptiness, loneliness, and regret. Cynthia Heimel makes this point vividly by talking about celebrities:

> I pity [celebrities]. No, I do. The minute a person becomes a celebrity is the same minute he/she becomes a monster. Sylvester Stallone, Bruce Willis and Barbra Streisand were once perfectly pleasant human beings with whom you might lunch on a slow Tuesday afternoon. But now they have become supreme beings, and their wrath is awful. It's not what they had in mind . . . The night each of them became famous they wanted to shriek with relief. Finally! Now they were adored! Invincible! Magic! The morning after the night each of them became famous, they wanted to take an overdose of barbiturates.
>
> All their fantasies had been realized, yet the reality was still the same. If they were miserable before, they were twice as miserable now, because that giant thing they were striving for, that fame thing that was going to make everything okay, that was going to make their lives bearable, that was going to provide them with personal fulfillment and (ha ha) happiness, had happened.
>
> And nothing changed. They were still them. The disillusionment turned them howling and insufferable.
> —*If You Can't Live Without Me, Why Aren't You Dead?*, p. 13.

Acknowledging God as God and rejecting all counterfeits is the chief challenge and defining purpose of our lives. Paradoxically, this is the only desire that, by God's own design, seeks something other than fulfillment. When we pursue this desire, we experience assurance that God is connecting the dots of our lives—even though we may not see it at the moment.

Being More

Earlier in this chapter I said that desire is the third rail of the soul. Our power to accomplish things and to make a contribution in life is derived from our passion. But along with this power comes the danger of spiritual electrocution. Our desires drive us to one of two destinations: larger life or destruction. My suggestion is simple. Desire is about "more"; to get on the right track to larger life and avoiding destruction, we must get "more" right.

Some people assume that getting "more" right involves finding the key to contentment. We hear a lot of advice about how to feel we have enough and how to avoid a sense of deprivation in folksy proverbs such as, "The key to happiness is not to have what you want, but to want what you have," or, "Don't try to fill the God-shaped hole in your heart with things that cannot fill it." These sayings warn us to avoid the temptation to pursue destructive objects of desire, and to keep our desires within reasonable limits. This is good advice, but it routinely ignores a kind of paradox. We are finite beings who want to receive the infinite love of the infinite God. To oversimplify for a moment, we are not big enough to receive the very thing God designed us to receive in order to know the joy he intends for us—and we never will be. God will always have more love than we are able to receive.

Our desire for God is our most fundamental desire. Etched into it is our desire to become something more, so that we can receive God ever more expansively into our lives. As the Psalmist says, "As the deer longs for streams of water, so I long for you, O God" (Psalm 42:1). This is not to say that God is holding himself back from us and leaving us suffering from spiritual thirst. This is a different sort of longing. Ronald Rohlheiser calls it a "holy longing." We desire chiefly to *be* more, not to *have* more. God has already given us himself, without reservation. The Holy Spirit dwells in the heart of every believer. We long to become more, so that God can dwell more fully in our lives. (Romans 8:11; 1 Corinthians 6:19; Ephesians 1:13–14; John 14:16)

But we frequently misinterpret this desire. Too many of us fear that we do not measure up, that God is waiting for us to make ourselves something more. Religious people sometimes get the Gospel wrong by assuming that we need to accumulate more moral achievements. Here is the good news: only God can make us into more, and that is just what he does. One of the chief works of the Holy Spirit is to stretch us to make more room for God in our lives. That is the very thing we desire.

Unlike any of our other desires, our desire for God is a delight in itself. If we pursue God in an attempt to acquire something else, then we are not really pursuing God. Also, our desire for God delights him. When we offer our lives to the glory of God, we at once pursue and receive what we desire the most. By giving ourselves away, in even our simplest, most routine activities, we receive the object of our deepest desire. Only by emptying ourselves are we genuinely fulfilled.

Desiring God for God

God desires more for us than just the fleeting contentment of possessions, entertainment, and applause. Our earthly comfort, security, and fulfillment are gifts from God, but they are not what he most wants for us. In fact, for the sake of our eternal relationship with him and with all of his children, God is willing to make us what many people would call unhappy. Regret, frustration, heartache, and even pain can be God's instruments for the redemption of our lives. His infinitely good plan for us is the fathomless joy of a seamless relationship with him. But this is possible only when we refuse to substitute God for something else.

When we make the pursuit of happiness our highest purpose, we end up viewing God as only an instrument to getting what we want: in this case, earthly goods. Jesus addressed the importance of desiring God for God, not merely as a means to something else, when he spoke to the crowd that chased him down, wanting to make him king after he'd fed them all with his miraculously multiplying loaves: "Truly, truly, I say to you, you are seeking me, not because you saw signs, but because you ate your fill of the loaves. Do not labor for the food that perishes, but for the food that endures to eternal life, which the Son of Man will give to you" (John 6:26–27). In other words: "You don't want me. You only want the stuff I can give you."

Enjoying a seamless relationship with God and having perfect fellowship with his children does not happen in this life. God has set us on a pilgrimage to life after this life, which only Jesus Christ can give us. We tend to lose sight of our true destination, and to suffer the miserable disappointment that inevitably follows by expecting this life to be the new heaven and the new earth, by expecting all the dots to be connected right now. God does not promise us uninterrupted contentment in this life. On the contrary, God may at certain times lead us to frustration, disappointment, obstacles, and detours precisely because they are the cure we need for our spiritual shortsightedness.

So how, you might ask, do we keep our focus on the new heaven and the new earth? We will not shape our lives with hope by merely saying no to our earthly idols. We must replace our pursuit of status and material things and experiences with a vivid love for Jesus. A vague belief in the existence of God will not suffice. God's love for us and our devotion to God must be a pulsing reality for us. For an example of this, consider Jesus' baptism (Mark 1:9–15). When he emerged from the water, he heard the Father say, "You are my Son, the Beloved; with you I am well pleased" (Mark 1:11). Through Jesus, we can all hear these words.

Imagine the power of hearing and feeling those words with your every breath and every heartbeat, and in every context, whether harrowing or hilarious, exhilarating or exhausting. "You are my beloved. I delight in you." When you hear this, your heart leaps. That is why Paul said, "Rejoice in the Lord always!" (Philippians 4:4). Make Christ your greatest treasure and free yourself from the tyranny of fleeting comforts and passing entertainments.

Rejoicing in Christ does not crowd good things out; it simply puts things in proper perspective. If we previously have made idols of earthly things, the answer is not to now start hating beautiful things or good food or successful careers. Instead, learn to love Christ so much more than these things that they can no longer hold you captive.

So how do we do this? How do we rejoice in Christ, in all that we do? We do it by remembering foremost what Jesus did for us on the cross. As St. Peter said, "Christ also suffered for sins once for all, the righteous for the unrighteous, in order to bring you to God" (1 Peter 3:18). Worship, personal prayer, Bible study, works of mercy, and sharing the Gospel are the means by which the Holy Spirit makes Christ a living reality in our daily experience. We see the Lord on the cross and realize with our hearts, not just our minds, that the wounds on his tortured back and the nails in his hands and feet are connecting the dots for us. We hear him say, "I have done this for you. You are my beloved." Only in this extravagant love will we find the happiness we seek. By experiencing his love for us, we are assured that he is connecting the dots of our lives.

Chapter Three

A Life that Matters

This life is a work in progress. It is never finished. And yet, followers of Jesus Christ believe that God is finishing it. He is connecting the dots. Hope shapes our lives, but in assuming a hopeful attitude, Jesus' followers are not sitting around doing nothing. On the contrary, we followers believe that what we do in this life matters. We are not here by accident. God has sent us into this life with a role to play in his redeeming work. Even though followers of Jesus live by hope, God does not intend for us to merely bide our time on this earth until something better—the afterlife—comes along. Our belief in the new heaven and the new earth motivates and encourages us to do whatever good we can, in whichever corner of the world we find ourselves. We are assured that whatever we do in Christ's name is eternally significant. Our lives matters.

When God created the earth, it was good. Our sin has cracked it and turned it upside down. God is not one who walks off and discards what he started, so, instead of abandoning his creation, God set about redeeming it. His work of redemption began in the cross of Jesus Christ. He will complete that work when Christ comes again to judge the living and the dead, and to make a new heaven and a new earth.

In the meantime, here we are. We live in a fractured, upside-down world. God has something for us to do. He wants us to join him in turning things right side up. He does not expect us to do this on our own. In fact, he wants us to recognize that this is his work, and that we are participants by his grace. Strictly speaking, he could do it on his own, if he so intended. But by following his son, Jesus Christ, we have the opportunity to be his instruments. There are two ways in which we can be God's faithful instruments.

First, we can simply act in obedience to God's will in our routine comings and goings. Following Christ in our ordinary conduct shapes the world from a heavenly direction in ways that we may never fully see. Of course, Jesus himself instructs us to serve the poor and to make disciples, but I am referring to more than this. When we obey God's direction in the routines of our daily lives, it is as if heaven infiltrates earth. Heroic, saintly acts provide encouragement and examples for believers. But God nudges the earth in a heavenly direction when we obediently change a baby's diapers, do small kindnesses for a neighbor, smile at the clerk at the deli counter, and countless other ordinary things

Our prayers also participate in turning the world right side up. Jesus promised that he would answer the prayers of the faithful, but he did not mean that God would be our heavenly vending machine or our celestial butler. Rather, our prayers are like conduits through which the power of God flows. When we pray for the restoration of a rocky marriage, for an addict's sobriety, for the healing of the sick, or for peace in time of war, God goes to work in and through those prayers.

God connects the dots of our personal lives and of the creation as a whole through our obedience to him in ordinary life and through our faithful prayers. Practically speaking, then, we have to find out what God wants us to do. The first portion of this chapter addresses this question: How do we discern God's will in our daily lives? The second part of this chapter takes up another question: How do we know that prayer really works? We will begin looking at the first question in the following section.

Bossypants

My wife Joy recently read *Bossypants*, Tina Fey's memoir about being a media boss. I have not yet read the book, but Tina Fey usually cracks me up. And that is one great title: *Bossypants*. It makes me chuckle. It has given me a new nickname for my wife (used in jest, really). Oddly enough, it has also made me think about how we approach our daily lives with hope. We pray, "Thy will be done on earth as it is in heaven." Being hopeful means aligning our will with God's will in the course of each day. But does that mean that we should view God as a sort of cosmic Bossypants? If Christian discipleship is all about being hopeful in this sense, does that mean that we should look for direction from Bossypants before we do anything at all?

Looking for a spouse? Wait for a word from Bossypants!

Thinking of buying a house? Wait for a word from Bossypants!

Considering a career change? Wait for a word from Bossypants!

Looking at a menu? Wait for a word from Bossypants!

Years ago, a man approached me about serving God in his life. He came to me again and again, asking the same thing. He insisted on hearing God's specific direction for his life before engaging in a ministry. The waiting had not ended by the time I left to serve another congregation. After several such visits, I started to think about Samuel Beckett's play *Waiting for Godot*. In it, the two characters, Estragon and Vladimir, are convinced that Godot (or God) is drawing near. They spend the entire play waiting for him to appear. He never comes, and they never do anything.

Don't get me wrong. I am all for following God's will, even though I do not always find it easy or comfortable or perfectly clear. My own need for regular repentance testifies to the fact that I miss the mark more often than I'd like to admit. But what does it mean to follow God's will? How do you know what he wants you to do?

Surely following God's will cannot mean waiting for crystal-clear mystical experiences that will provide unmistakable direction for every single thing in life. That would be like a reality show called *Waiting for Bossypants* where nothing ever happens. Neither can it mean tossing responsibility for our choices onto God. Your ex-girlfriend wants an explanation for your breakup? It wasn't your fault, it was God's will. You quit your job in the middle of a crucial project to take an offer from your main competition? Not your fault. God's will.

Several recent books explore what we mean by "God's will," and what it means to follow his will. Kevin DeYoung's *Just Do Something* is entirely devoted to this subject. Philip Cary's *Good News for Anxious Christians* focuses largely on this subject, and Oliver Thomas's *10*

Things Your Minister Wants to Tell You! also touches on it. Gregory Boyd discusses God's providence and our free will in *Is God to Blame?* and *God of the Possible*. For now, let's just outline what we might mean by "God's will."

For starters, we have the idea of Providence. God moves all things according to his plan to redeem the creation. You can resist God's will, protest God's will, hate God's will, or be indifferent to God's will, but it does not matter; regardless, this is how things are going to turn out. God is the absolute Sovereign.

Next, there is God's law. God commands us to behave in certain ways. We are moral beings because we have minds capable of understanding God's clear imperatives, and we have the freedom to refuse to obey God's commands. Following God's law means doing what we know is right. Holy Scripture and the traditional teachings of the Christian faith guide us to know what is right. God gave us minds so that we could learn these moral principles and wills, and obey them. God's good is eternal and immutable.

Finally, there is God's plan for your life. This is where things get sticky. Does God have a specific career in mind for me? A specific job? What about a spouse? Children? Which physician? Which brand of dental floss? For the most part, these are morally neutral matters. Kevin DeYoung advises us to stop thinking of God's plan for our lives as a corn maze to find our way through. Corn-maze thinking looks like this: make all the right turns and you are blessed, but take the wrong turn and you are celestially lost. Instead, we must remember all those pages in the Bible devoted to wisdom. As Paul said, "Do not be conformed to this world, but be transformed by the renewal of your mind, that by testing you may discern what is the will of God, what is good and acceptable and perfect" (Romans 12:2). Or, to cite Proverbs: "Blessed is the one who finds wisdom, and the one who gets understanding" (Proverb 3:13).

Following Jesus involves a life devoted to worship and study. Jesus is our Savior. He is also our supreme and reliable teacher. Sitting at his feet, we gradually learn to think like him. If you have been fortunate enough to have a mentor in school or at work, you might already have had an experience like this. The point of mentorship is not just to make us agree on the facts. Mentors teach us *how* to think, not just *what* to think.

God's plan is for us to gain wisdom by following his Son. For the most part, he does not give us a detailed road map of what to do. Neither does intend his supposed silence to be interpreted as instruction for inaction. Even less does he want us to shirk responsibility for our decisions by saying God made us do a thing that other people did not like. We all make mistakes, but at every point of our lives, God himself is actively involved. He not only nudges us, but also nags us and points us in certain directions. He also wants us to grow in wisdom and to make godly decisions for which we are fully responsible.

Wisdom

Lots of people are principled. They follow a code of ethics or adhere to a philosophy of life. Christian discipleship is different. We do not follow a code; we follow a person. We follow Jesus Christ, and we believe that he gives us direction for our lives. He gives us not only general principles to guide us, but also specific guidance and even commands for the ordinary conduct of our daily lives. And what an advantage this is.

You follow a code or a set of principles because it is the right thing to do, or because it gives you the highest probability of success. We follow Jesus because he is in this life with us and for us; he knows us personally and knows the paths we should take to arrive at the infinite good that he wants for us. Let's understand how involved God gets in the details and specifics of our daily lives, and how we can find out what God wants us to do.

God's involvement is total. He wants to be part of every moment of every day of every month of every year of our lives. Remember that Jesus told us, "Are not two sparrows sold for a penny? And not one of them will fall to the ground apart from your Father. But even the hairs of your head are all numbered. Fear not, therefore; you are of more value than many sparrows" (Matthew 10:29–31). God does not sit back passively and just note the details. He does not merely watch and keep score, waiting for us to stumble so that he can condemn us. He walks slightly ahead of us in life, so that he can give us a heads up about when to turn, when to stop, and when to go straight.

He is not interested in annihilating our power of choice. He is dedicated to guiding our choices. God is interested in our spouses, our parenting, the quality of our work, which jobs we take and which we decline, where we live, and even whether we floss our teeth regularly. And yet, God is not a control freak. He is our wise Creator, Lord, Judge, and Redeemer. God's involvement in our lives is just practice for eternity. After all, God made us in his image. He made us for an eternity with him up close and personal. God directs our actions every day, because when we are in step with him can we become all that we can be. Now let's look at what it means to get direction from God.

Some people seem to expect God to speak to them as he spoke to Moses. God appeared to Moses in a burning bush whose flames did not consume it. He made his presence unmistakably clear so that Moses would know without a doubt that it was God who was speaking. He gave Moses very specific orders to go to Egypt. God had heard his people's cries, and he was in their corner. Moses was God's representative in the largest rescue mission the world had ever seen. If you read the rest of Exodus and Numbers, you will see that this pattern continues. God repeatedly tells Moses exactly what to do: hold up your staff at the Red Sea, strike that rock for water, follow these pillars of cloud and fire. Step by step, he tells Moses how to get the Israelites to the Promised Land.

Lots of Christians (and other non-Christian but spiritual people) pray to God to give them a sign or to tell them what to do concerning big issues. They are looking for some version of the burning bush. Even denominations that emphasize the authority of reason, like the Episcopal Church, talk about listening for the guidance of the Spirit. Sometimes God does give us burning bushes and actually tells us what he wants us to do. But this is very rare, and for good reason. The voices we hear in our hearts are very hard to sort out. Is it your own fleeting desire? A demonic suggestion? A divine inspiration? Or just mental indigestion? Don't get me wrong; I believe that the Holy Spirit reveals all truth, and actively moves in our lives. I have even heard, in an odd, indescribable way, the voice of God in my heart. But like the burning bush, this was an exceptional experience, not to be sought out every day. If we do dwell on those inner voices, we are all too likely to kid ourselves into believing that God is telling us to do something when in fact it, we are just thinking about what we, ourselves, want to do.

God can still speak to us in mystical ways, but he mostly speaks to us through Holy Scripture.

There are several ways that he guides us through the Bible. The Bible gives us clear moral laws. The Ten Commandments are a perfect example.

> Keep the Sabbath holy.
> Honor your mother and father.
> Do not murder and do not steal.

These laws and others like them tell us explicitly what to do and what to avoid doing. They are given to us by God, so by obeying them, we stay in step with God. But merely obeying the law produces only a distant kind of relationship, and does not drill down deep into our daily, personal lives. Though we might get frustrated or angry with our loved ones, we would not actually plan to kill them. If we focused solely on following the law, we would live as though God had merely given us broad marching orders from a distance, and was going to look in on us from time to time just to make certain we were staying in line. No, God wants to get closer to us, and he does.

Jesus said to his disciples, "If anyone would come after me, let him deny himself and take up his cross and follow me. For whoever would save his life will lose it, but whoever loses his life for my sake will find it" (Matthew 16:24–25). This is not just a list of dos and don'ts; it is a lesson about how to live every moment of our lives. Jesus is talking about our attitudes, our goals, and our behaviors in every kind of situation that might arise. He is telling us how to deal with moral dilemmas, but also with ordinary parts of life: marriage, raising kids, jobs to take and to quit.

We hear what he says as our teacher, and we think, "Can you tell me exactly what that means? How do I do that?" How do we take up the cross in our marriages, our parenting, our jobs, at the voting booth, at the market, and behind the steering wheel? Should I listen more carefully to my wife, or tell her the truth about that thing that drives me nuts? Should I push my kids to achieve, or just lighten up on them? Jesus understood that his disciples would need wisdom to apply all of his teachings. Whether they be parables, beatitudes, or apocalyptic prophesies, Jesus gave us his teachings as directions for daily living.

Wisdom requires that we know what Jesus said, but it also involves the next step. Wisdom is the ability to see which of Jesus' teachings illuminates the situation you find yourself in, and what action that teaching calls for.

We accrue wisdom by spending time faithfully studying the Scriptures. As it says in Proverbs,

> My son, if you receive my words and treasure up my commandments with you making your ear attentive to wisdom and inclining your heart to understanding; yes, if you call out for insight and raise your voice for understanding, if you seek it like silver and search for it as for hidden treasures, then you will understand the fear of the Lord and find the knowledge of God. For the Lord gives wisdom; from his mouth come knowledge and understanding.
> —Proverbs 2:1–6

Jesus is the Word of God (John 1:1). All the words of the Bible ultimately point us back to the Word of God. Spending time with the Bible as people of faith, submitting ourselves to its truth and correction, is one of the principal ways that we spend time with Jesus Christ.

Without quantity, there is no quality time with Jesus either. It takes much time to impart wisdom. Through the power of the Holy Spirit, Jesus teaches us how to think, perceive, respond, will, and even feel like he does. This is what Paul means when he talks about taking on the mind of Christ (1 Corinthians 2:16). Paul said in Romans, "Do not be conformed to this world, but be transformed by the renewal of your mind, that by testing you may discern what is the will of God, what is good and acceptable and perfect" (Romans 12:2).

Though the analogy is imperfect, I am reminded of my dissertation director, Dr. Rudolf Makkreel. Rudi scrutinized every line of every chapter of my dissertation. He then sat with me and went over every unclear passage, every weak argument, every suspect interpretation, and every questionable translation. By spending time with me and wrestling intellectually with me, Rudi Makkreel taught me to read carefully, to think critically, to write precisely, and to render interpretations on solid evidence. In other words, Rudi did not merely teach me what to think; he taught me how to think like a philosopher and an intellectual historian.

Jesus teaches us the truth about God's will for us, but he also imparts wisdom. By spending time with us, his ways of thinking, feeling, willing, imagining, and perceiving rub off on us. Wisdom alone will not save us. Jesus does not teach us wisdom so that we can get by without him. In fact, at the beginning and the end of wisdom is the understanding that we are utterly dependent upon the mercy of God, and that the merciful God is with us in this life, through thick and thin. As it is written in Proverbs, "The fear of the Lord is the beginning of wisdom" (Proverb 9:10).

Jesus' clearest, most fundamental direction to each of us is that he has come to give us the mercy we need and desire. He has come to deliver us from our bondage to sin and sorrow, suffering and death. He has come to guide us in marriage and parenting, in work and play, in good times and hard times. Moses knew that God was speaking because of the miraculous burning bush. We know that the only Son is speaking because he speaks from the cross. He speaks eternal life from the midst of an instrument of death. "Father, forgive them, for they know not what they do" (Luke 23:34). When we hear his words with the wisdom he has taught us, we can face any challenge, any obstacle, any enemy with the bold confidence that, in Jesus Christ, we will be more than conquerors (Romans 8:35–39). By God's direction, we are working with him to nudge the world to its tipping point.

It may be difficult to see that our everyday obedience contributes to setting the world right side up. It is even more difficult for some to see how prayer can change anything in the world. Yet this is precisely what Christians believe: prayer changes things.

Does Prayer Work?

Jesus himself instructs us to pray. Moreover, he promises that when we gather together as a body, the Father will answer our prayers. He says, "If two of you agree on earth about anything they ask, it will be done for them by my Father in heaven" (Matthew 18:19). Jesus tells us that he is the truth and that we can stake our very lives on his promises (John 14:6; 5:24–27; 6:40).

Just as Jesus promised, many of us have experienced having our prayers answered. We have probably all experienced unanswered prayers, too. We may doubt Jesus' words about prayer when our prayers seem to fall on deaf ears. This poses a serious problem. If we cannot believe him about prayer, then why should we believe his words about the forgiveness of our sins or the hope of eternal life? If he were mistaken or untruthful about one thing, then what he says about other things might also be unreliable, and an unreliable Savior is no Savior at all. Skepticism about prayer undermines our ability to trust Jesus Christ, so having a reasonable account of how God answers our prayers is not a theological sideshow. It touches the very heart of our faith. It is no wonder, then, that we Christians are sometimes too hasty to explain what appear to be unanswered prayers. Here are a couple of common explanations that miss the mark. You have probably heard them, or at least a variation on these themes.

This first common misconception is that God does not answer prayers unless you are faithful enough. There is supposedly a sort of faith threshold you must cross before God will respond to prayers. Minor league faith does not warrant God's notice. So, if you have prayed for a loved one's recovery from an illness to no avail, or if you prayed to get a job that you desperately need but did not even get an interview, then only you are to blame; you are not faithful enough. In truth, Jesus Himself said that even faith the size of a mustard seed will do remarkable things. And let's face it, you would not pray at all unless you did have a grain of faith.

Here is another unsatisfying explanation for apparently unanswered prayers. God did respond to those prayers; He just said no. As we will see, this is closer to the mark, but it fails to match either the letter or the spirit of Jesus' own teaching. Jesus said explicitly that the Father will do whatever we ask in agreement with each other. There is no denying that things often do not turn out the way we expect or want. However, it is important for us to see how what may seem like a no from God is in fact an undiluted yes.

This first step in adjusting our theological lenses is to clear away some basic misconceptions that distort our understanding of prayer. This is the topic of the next section. I will show you that we are the victims of a case of mistaken identity. We can be mistaken about who we really are.

Mistaken Identity

Let's begin by taking Jesus at his word. God does not answer our prayers by saying yes sometimes and no other times. When two or three of Jesus' disciples agree in prayer, God grants their petition. Let's right away dismiss the idea that Jesus was only talking to the hyper-faithful among his followers. He was, in fact, addressing disciples who routinely misunderstood him and said embarrassingly stupid things, and who eventually abandoned him when he most needed their friendship (Mark 8:14–17; 9:33–34; 14:50). This means that God is answering your prayers and my prayers even when it does not seem like he is. The problem lies in how we see things, not in what God is doing in our lives.

Something is distorting and obscuring our vision. Our problem is a case of mistaken identity. We have misconstrued who we are and what our purpose is in this life, and as a result, misunderstand who God is and the role that prayer plays in our relationship with God. So, who do we think we are and why do we think we are here? We think that we are self-reliant and self-governing. To use a more philosophical phrase, we consider ourselves autonomous agents. We stand on our own two feet. We shape our lives by the choices we freely make.

Some who hold this view argue that the point of human life is happiness. For the most part, by happiness, they mean earthly well-being: good feelings, physical comforts, career success, and warm family relationships. In other words, the choices we make are guided by the pursuit of happiness as our highest goal. Others insist that the point of this life is actually the next life. The moral quality of our choices determines whether we will enter heaven or hell after this life is over. The choices we make are governed by our desire for eternal salvation. Whether we are pursuing the good life or eternal life, we still think of the pursuit as being principally our own, and of God's activity an intervention in the ordinary course of events, or simply as a judgment after everything has been said and done. This perspective gives us only three possible and unsatisfactory approaches to prayer.

The first approach is Instrumental Prayer. We pray to God only to get something for ourselves or for someone else. The problem is that we only reach out to God for what he can do for us or get for us; we do not love God for who he is. He is just an instrument for pursuing our own agendas.

Let's call the next unsatisfactory approach Resignation Prayer. Recognizing that God's will is sovereign, we bring our fears, concerns, and needs to him, but always end each prayer with the phrase, "Thy will be done." The problem is not that we desire to align our will with God's; this is, in fact, a good thing. The problem is that into we express, in pious words, a deep suspicion that God does not really care about the tender specifics of our lives. We have already resigned ourselves that God will not do anything for us unless it happens to be on his own agenda. This is resignation, not faith.

Finally, we have Self-Transforming Prayer. This is especially common among people who loudly classify themselves as spiritual but not religious. Prayer is a spiritual exercise that helps us to change our own souls. It is a means of spiritual growth that we apply to ourselves, like transcendental meditation. The problem is that prayer makes us focus on ourselves, not on giving ourselves away as a living sacrifice, as Paul talked about in Romans 12:1. We spend our energies on self-transformation rather than on connecting more deeply with God.

Each of these approaches misses the point of prayer because it is based on a misconception of who we really are. We are not autonomous agents; we are extremely dependent beings. As followers of Jesus Christ, we are people with a mission. Jesus himself sent us into the world to continue the mission he began. This fact is the key to understanding that God always answers the prayers of the faithful. The connection between who we are and prayer is our next subject.

Speaking and Hearing

I grew up with a speech impediment. I was born with a cleft palate, physically incapable of making the "s" sound. The condition required two surgeries. I received one of those in my infancy. In my early twenties, a surgeon completed the repair, and I uttered normal speech for the first time.

Years of garbled speech presented various challenges for me, but they also provided me with an analogy of prayer. When I spoke, most people had difficulty understanding me. I could not make myself clear.

Some felt uneasy around me, because it is awkward to be forever asking someone to repeat himself. (My rough edges did not help much either, to be honest.) But there were people who had a knack for understanding me with apparently no extra effort. They could hear through what I garbled to the meaning I wanted to convey. Our prayers are like garbled speech. We cannot make ourselves clear. But God can and does respond to our meanings even when we fail to make our messages clear.

Before we continue, I do want to emphasize that this analogy is limited. When I spoke to others as a young man, I knew very well what I was trying to say. My speech was garbled, not my thoughts. In contrast, our prayers often arise from limited perspectives, distorted desires, and confused thinking. If we consider intercessory prayer to be us crying out to God, then our speech is garbled at many levels. Nevertheless, God hears what we mean. He hears the genuine needs and longings that motivate our prayers, and he responds with a resounding yes. God always answers our prayers.

We have to be clear about who we are as speakers in order to understand that God always answers the prayers of the faithful. There are three things to know about us: We are finite, we are fallen, and we are followers of Jesus. Let's look at each of these in turn.

We are finite. God created us with the gift of intellect, but our reason is not infinite. We cannot know everything. Even the biggest big picture we can see is only a partial perspective of the whole of creation. We may see glimpses of God's plan for each life and for the destiny of creation, but the details remain clouded in mystery. Think about what God said when Job challenged him to explain suffering. "Where were you when I laid the foundation of the earth? Tell me, if you have understanding. Who determined its measurements—surely you know! Or who stretched the line upon it? On what were its bases sunk, or who laid its cornerstone, when the morning stars sang together and all the sons of God shouted for joy?" (Job 38:4–6).

We will always offer prayers from a partial, imperfect perspective. With intercessory prayers, we bring our deep needs and tender longings to God. But because we are finite, we may not clearly know how we could meet those needs or satisfy those longings. We may even have trouble identifying the true nature of our longings. But God has an acute sense of hearing. He hears our prayers more clearly than we are able to plead them. He addresses the needs we bring to him even when we ask for things that would not do us any good in the end. God grants us good that we do not even know how to ask for.

Sometimes, in retrospect, we can see that God's apparent refusal to answer our prayers was in fact him answering with a yes" A friend of mine was unemployed for about a year. He prayed fervently for a job, and other members of the church also prayed for him regularly. Early on, he attended several job interviews in his chosen field, but they did not lead anywhere. Eventually, there were no more interviews. It began gradually to dawn on him that his spiritual issue was not his unemployment. In fact, he had spent his life working for all the wrong reasons. His career had been a means of justifying his own existence. In the midst of unemployment, he came to see that his infinite worth derived from the cross, not from his own achievements. When this realization took firm hold of him, he received a job offer in a field that I will simply describe as servant ministry. He has never felt more fulfilled. This is a happy example, but unfortunately, not every such case comes with a retrospective explanation. Many of us are left aching from a broken relationship or the loss of a loved one. Acknowledging that we are finite does not diminish such struggles, but it does give us a framework for persevering in hope by relying on God.

We are fallen. God created us in his image. This means that God created us to desire the good that resembles him. his original plan was that our prayers would reflect God's purposes for his creation. As children of the fall, we bear the marks of Adam's fateful decision. We inherit faulty spiritual DNA. To borrow a phrase from William Stafford, we are inhabited by disordered loves. What we want and crave can be debasing to others and destructive to ourselves. Neither baptism nor conversion completely restore us to our original states. What theologians call sanctification happens gradually, over time. The Holy Spirit transforms us (often in the midst of prayer itself) into the image of Christ, but usually in baby steps. So once again, we find ourselves offering garbled prayers to God. We can bring to God things unworthy of him and his kingdom even while thinking that we are bringing things that are good.

Offering examples of this sort of prayer is a little tricky, so I will play it safe and refer to the Psalms. Listen to the ghastly prayer offered by those suffering through the Babylonian captivity: "O daughter of Babylon, doomed to be destroyed, blessed shall he be who repays you with what you have done to us! Blessed shall he be who takes your little ones and dashes them against the rock!" (Psalms 137:8–9). Some say you should be careful what you pray for, because God may grant your destructive request. Watch out! But this is not true. God did not dash the captors' little ones against the rocks to satisfy the Israelites' distorted desire for vengeance. Instead, he heard, in their harsh words and tortured passion, their deeper cries for deliverance and justice, and God gave them deliverance and justice. He brought the Israelites out of captivity and restored Jerusalem. God can hear through our garbled prayers to the desires and loves that we were designed to have. God says yes to these loves every time.

Finally, in addition to being finite and fallen, we are followers—followers of Jesus Christ. This is more important than being either finite or fallen.

Disciples and Ambassadors

God answers our prayers. But if he simply granted the things we actually asked for, then we might say to him what St. Teresa of Avila told him when she fell from her donkey into the mud: "If this is the way you treat your friends, no wonder you have so few of them!" As I have explained, our prayers are always imperfect. We are finite, so we pray in ignorance of the big picture that only God can see. In addition, we are fallen. Sometimes our prayers arise from disordered desires and misguided motives. God clearly and compassionately hears our needs and our yearning for our highest good. God filters through the garbled messages we send him and arrives at the true petition that we may only dimly comprehend. There is yet more to consider when we say that God answers our prayers. In addition to being finite and fallen, we are also followers of Jesus Christ. We will look at the difference this makes in a moment. But let's emphasize a few things first.

We are not autonomous beings. Whether or not we are Christians, we are radically dependent upon God for every nanosecond of our existence. God literally wills us into being at every moment. Otherwise, we simply would not *be*. Earthly contentment is not the point of life. God is not against material comforts and personal success—these things are fine as far as they go. But God wants more for us. He wants us to enjoy perfect reconciliation with him, and as a result of that, perfect reconciliation with each other. We are broken. Our relationship with our maker is broken. Our relationships with each other are broken. Our hearts are broken. Healing all of this brokenness is God's single-minded purpose. He will connect all the dots. He will let nothing stand in his way, not even our earthly ease and serenity.

So then, what are we doing on this planet? Paul said that Jesus Christ came to bring the ministry of reconciliation and that we followers are now ambassadors of reconciliation. "Therefore, if anyone is in Christ, he is a new creation. The old has passed away; behold, the new has come. All this is from God, who through Christ reconciled us to himself and gave us the ministry of reconciliation; that is, in Christ God was reconciling the world to himself, not counting their trespasses against them, and entrusting to us the message of reconciliation. Therefore, we are ambassadors for Christ, God making his appeal through us" (2 Corinthians 5:17–20).

Think for a moment about what ambassadors do. The appropriate sovereign authority of a country—in the United States this is the president, with the agreement of Congress—appoints and sends diplomats to other countries to serve as representatives of their own country. An ambassador's authority comes from the government that sent him or her. Ambassadors perform a variety of official functions, but I will focus on just one of them: ambassadors extend greetings from their political leaders to a foreign leader.

Imagine that the American ambassador meets the Ugandan ambassador and says, "I greet you in the name of the president of the United States." The American ambassador's words are not merely reporting or describing something; they are doing something. By saying, "I greet you," the ambassador accomplishes greeting the Ugandan ambassador on behalf of the American president. Philosophers call this kind of speech performative. J. L. Austin introduced the idea in the book *How to Do Things with Words*. Philosophy instructors often use wedding vows as an example. When the bride and groom say, "I do," they make something happen: they tie the knot.

Now let's go back to the idea that we are ambassadors for Christ. Heaven has selected us and sent us into the world. Through not only our actions, but also our prayers, we are doing something world-changing. When we pray, we speak on behalf of the Sovereign who has chosen and sent us. We are not working on our own initiative or on the basis of our own authority, nor are our words just reporting. When we pray, we are responding to God's initiative; he sets the earth right side up through our prayers. Our prayers unleash on earth what God has already begun in heaven.

Our prayers, words, and actions can be misguided, half-hearted, or fumbling, but God promises He will take even our feeblest efforts and use them to achieve his purposes. Consider the words of St. Paul: "Likewise the Spirit helps us in our weakness. For we do not know what to pray for as we ought, but the Spirit himself intercedes for us with groanings too deep for words. And he who searches hearts knows what is the mind of the Spirit, because the Spirit intercedes for the saints according to the will of God. And we know that for those who love God all things work together for good, for those who are called according to his purpose" (Romans 8:26–28). If we pray for something stupid, harmful, or shortsighted, God does not use that against us. His loving mercy always takes what we give him in faith and works it for the good he intends for us. On the cross, even our sins become the seedbed of eternal life.

Okay, you might be saying, then why does it look like so many worthy prayers go unanswered? Children are starving. Innocents die in ethnic violence. Despots oppress whole populations. People we know personally suffer from disease, loneliness, and addiction. We end up burying loved ones, despite our most fervent prayers for their healing. Our righteous indignation and sorrow and longing are not misplaced, but neither are they signs that our prayers have been for nothing. Our disappointment and confusion arise because we mistakenly think the prayers we utter should work like switches or magic wands, instantly resolving tensions, healing broken hearts, and mending relationships. We expect earth to be the new heaven and the new earth, right now. It is not yet, but God is using our prayers to bring about the perfect reconciliation he promises. He teaches us to endure and persevere in faith, for there is much work left to be done.

Consider yourself an ambassador in wartime working in occupied territory. Enemy forces are dead set against God's purposes. You greet them and sign a treaty, but they reject the greeting and tear up the treaty. This does not mean that your prayer did not work. Your prayer is part of God's creation of the new heaven and the new earth. You are changing the world in ways that you cannot yet see. To return to the guiding metaphor of this book, God is connecting the dots through our prayers. We cannot yet see the final picture that God will produce, but our hope inspires us to pray without ceasing.

CHAPTER FOUR

HOPE AMID THE WEEDS

It may seem paradoxical, but assuming a hopeful posture requires us to be remarkably practical. The followers of Jesus trust in God's promise to redeem his creation. As a result, we are emboldened to face reality on its own, often heart-rending, terms. There is much good in the world we inhabit, yet there is evil as well. Naming and facing and even struggling against evil in this life all come with being hopeful. One of the challenges we face is how to distinguish good and evil.

Some people insist that a bright line separates good and evil. They believe there is a war going on between the two opposing forces, and that all people stand on one side or the other of that line. For instance, I once presided at the funeral of a murdered police officer. The chief of police spoke at the funeral. He said that there were good people and evil people, and that police officers formed the barrier protecting us good people from unimaginably malevolent forces.

Most progressive and postmodern intellectuals consider this sort of talk unsophisticated; they would classify it as black-and-white thinking. They believe that life is composed of various shades of gray. Good and evil are labels arising from fear of differences and desire to control. From their perspective, moral reasoning is a tool of oppression and marginalization. An enlightened mind is *Beyond Good and Evil*, to borrow the title of Friedrich Nietzsche's famous work.

Many Christians sincerely believe some variation on one of these two extreme views of good and evil, yet they are not what Jesus taught. Let's start by hearing out Jesus himself. The following is often called the Parable of the Wheat and the Tares, or The Wheat and the Weeds.

> He put before them another parable: 'The kingdom of heaven may be compared to someone who sowed good seed in his field; but while everybody was asleep, an enemy came and sowed weeds among the wheat, and then went away. So when the plants came up and bore grain, then the weeds appeared as well. And the slaves of the householder came and said to him, "Master, did you not sow good seed in your field? Where, then, did these weeds come from?" He answered, "An enemy has done this." The slaves said to him, "Then do you want us to go and gather them?" But he replied, "No; for in gathering the weeds you would uproot the wheat along with them. Let both of them grow together until the harvest; and at harvest time I will tell the reapers, Collect the weeds first and bind them in bundles to be burned, but gather the wheat into my barn."'
> —Matthew 13:24–30

The parable clearly distinguishes wheat and weeds to be respectively good and evil. At the time of harvest, God himself will sort them out. We humans lack the necessary skill or permission to eradicate evil. The root systems of wheat and weeds are so intertwined that uprooting the weeds would involve uprooting and destroying the wheat. Good and evil are so bound up with each other in ordinary human existence that we cannot eradicate one without destroying the other.

This is a far cry from saying that there is no black and white and that all is gray. This parable acknowledges that each and every one of us is mix of wheat and weeds. As Christians, we are to resist evil, yet we do not do so as people who have achieved righteousness by the power of our own will. In fact, each of us struggles with some sort of evil within (Romans 7:19). The cross of Christ redeems us. God has shown us mercy. We struggle with evil not as self-made righteous warriors with license to wreak havoc, but as redeemed sinners learning the power of God's mercy.

Spiritual Posture

How, then, do Christians confront evil in the world? One way to address this question is to consider the use of force. Can Christians justifiably kill bad guys? Can we even say that there are bad guys? Or to frame the question in a more precise way: many Christians, following Christian principles, legitimately use violence to stop evil? It's an old question. Reasonable attitudes range from unconditional pacifism to the just war theory. When a team of Navy SEALS killed Osama bin Laden, Christian commentators voiced opinions along this spectrum. Before wading into the fray about how Christians should respond to evil, I want to talk a bit about how to distinguish good from evil.

First, I want to talk about posture. Odd though it may sound, physical posture is a helpful metaphor for understanding spiritual posture, and good and evil are matters of spiritual posture. Good posture allows you to maintain your balance with minimum effort. It facilitates breathing and circulation. Good posture also suggests poise and grace, making you aesthetically pleasing. Just think how easy it is to spot a trained dancer in a crowd. In contrast, poor posture results in muscle pain, nerve pain, and constriction of blood flow. Whether or not it is fair, slouching connotes indifference, disrespect, and sloth. Notice here that I am talking about posture as your habit of holding your physical frame. I exclude congenital conditions like scoliosis and kyphosis.

Think of good posture as cooperating with gravity, holding yourself in a way that puts the least strain on your supporting muscles and ligaments. We sometimes slump in our chairs or walk with our shoulders hunched forward because we are tired, sad, or preoccupied. If this is the exception to usual habits, then we may suffer a little stiffness, but otherwise, suffer no harm. A problem arises when we make a habit of slouching and slumping and drooping and sagging. In time, these ways of standing and sitting will become second nature, and do lasting harm to our health, diminishing our quality of life and requiring medical intervention.

So, what does all of this have to do with good and evil? Let's start at the very beginning: the first chapter of Genesis. God created all that is, and saw that it was good. He created everything with the right posture toward him and toward everything else in his creation. God's moral law is less a set of discrete rules for separate actions as it is the principle by which everything hangs together. It is like gravity.

We humans can practice good posture. In other words, we can cooperate with divine gravity and hold ourselves habitually in a way that promotes wholeness and health. We can choose how we will stand and sit. However, we cannot choose to make bad spiritual posture result in a healthy spiritual condition. Gravity is gravity. Divine gravity pulls us toward right relation with the Creator and with fellow human beings. Bad spiritual posture amounts to turning yourself away from God and away from other people. It is a resistance to divine gravity, to the way of God. The result is an increasingly disfigured and tortured life. Here is where the metaphor begins to break down. My bad physical posture may be an eyesore to you, but in the end it won't hurt you. In contrast, spiritual posture by its very nature seeks to pull others down with it. Evil is destructive.

There is also an important catch here that figures prominently in how Christians respond to evil. You can do something about your bodily posture. Just check out the Internet for exercises to strengthen your core and to learn good standing and sitting habits. As far as our bodies go, we can straighten ourselves up. But the Gospel tells us that, spiritually, we start in a very different place. God does not stand at a distance waiting for us to straighten ourselves up. Instead, he sees clearly that our posture holds us captive. Paul put it famously in this passage: "For I do not do what I want, but I do the very thing I hate. Now if I do what I do not want, I agree that the law is good. But in fact it is no longer I that do it, but sin that dwells within me" (Romans 7:15–17). In other words, "My posture has gotten the better of me." Paul does not go on to provide seven steps to healthy spiritual posture. There are no self-help instructions in Romans or anywhere else in Paul's letters or the Gospels. Instead, Paul says, "Wretched man that I am! Who will rescue me from this body of death? Thanks be to God through Jesus Christ our Lord!" (Romans 7:24–25).

Just as divine gravity draws us toward the right posture toward God and others, forces beyond our control tip us toward destructive and self-destructive postures. The intervention of Jesus Christ and the power of the Holy Spirit make it possible for us to cooperate with God's gravity. Still, though, there are forces that will buffet us and push us toward a twisted bearing. As I will make clear, Jesus instructs his followers to resist falling under the sway of evil in our personal lives. He also rallies us to confront and combat the powers of evil in this world.

Before moving on to talk about how to actively oppose evil, I want to underscore one thing: we should not confuse our response to evil with our reactions to personal slights. Our hurt feelings, our injured pride, and our wounded souls are not the measure of someone else's evil. Redressing personal slights as opposing evil resembles revenge rather than justice. When we begin to respond to evil, we must be sure that we are confronting a spiritual posture that tears the fabric of God's creation. Evil is a posture that resists God and degrades and debases his children as a matter of ingrained habit.

Deliver Us from Evil

Jesus Christ is the Prince of Peace. Following his teachings and his example, Christians seek to settle conflict in nonviolent ways as a matter of principle. Nonviolence is our first choice, and we pursue it to the point that others might wonder at our sanity. Conflict often occurs between two good and reasonable parties whose points of view differ. Violence is never in order in those cases. In fact, well-managed, respectful conflict of this sort can lead to new insights and deepened relationships. But sometimes, conflict results from evil.

Evil is the anti-peace. Evil is utter resistance to God's order of things. God designed the universe to hang together like a *Luminous Web*, to borrow a Barbara Brown Taylor title. There is only God's order. Any divergence from or alteration of that order is destructive, and debases the life God intends for us. Evil promises an order that is more just, more lucrative, more pleasurable, or more vaguely free, but it merely tears apart the threads that hold together what God intends to be a peaceable kingdom. God calls upon Christians to resist evil. As a last resort, we may use violent means to stop the destructive forces of evil. Before I go on, I will here acknowledge that some will find this point of view completely unpersuasive. Our starting points are so out of synch that we will never reach the same conclusion.

If you do not believe there is such a thing as evil, if perhaps you think evil is what we call the things that threaten us in some way, then what I am about to say will seem to you utterly misguided. Or, perhaps, you are a pacifist relativist, and in your view, there is no absolute moral law, so there can't be such a thing as evil, either. However, you make an exception to your relativism: any harm done to others is wrong. Without an absolute moral law, I cannot see how one could pursue peace with moral zeal. But my point here is that you, too, will find what I am about to suggest unsophisticated and maybe even a little dim-witted.

But in contrast, if you routinely pray the Lord's Prayer and mean it, then you should at least be open to my suggestion. Remember, we pray, "Lead us not into temptation, but deliver us from evil." Jesus himself taught us to pray for deliverance from evil. Some will immediately respond with these words from Jesus: "All who take the sword will perish by the sword" (Matthew 26:52). It is true that all who strike out in anger, who seek nothing more than to settle a personal score, who inflict pain for the perverse pleasure of it, will be consumed by their own destructive ways. Nevertheless, violence can be used justly to protect the weak from evil. As the Psalmist said, "Rescue the weak and the needy; deliver them from the hand of the wicked" (Psalm 82:4).

Contrary to the faux wisdom of bumper stickers that insist waging war for the sake of peace is a contradiction in terms, it is not a contradiction to employ violence in order to achieve peaceful ends. The evidence for this rests in part on a remark made by Jesus that seems out of character for him: "Do not think that I have come to bring peace to the earth; I have not come to bring peace, but a sword" (Matthew 10:34). As Thomas Aquinas pointed out, Jesus is not interested in maintaining a superficial, illusory peace. That would be a kind of peace in which open hostilities have ceased, but there is still a constant threat of terror, and people cope in misery, or live with lies, or scurry to stay under the radar of oppressive, coercive powers. This is not the kind of peace that Jesus came to bring; He came to bring the final sword to a debased existence that equates peace with perpetual violence and a tolerable level of misery.

It may seem Christian to wait passively until the Lord himself eradicates evil, but as surely as he teaches us that we are his instruments in addressing poverty until he comes again (Matthew 25:31–46), so too does Jesus instruct us to struggle against evil, in his name. As Paul said, properly authorized violent means can serve God's just purposes (Romans 13:3–4).

Much has been written about the just war theory. Its basic principles have remained the same since Thomas Aquinas's day. Proper authorities must sanction violent means for the greater good; violence is never appropriate in the service of personal, self-interested feelings. In other words, we can justify violence only as a response to aggression against us or in defense of those who cannot defend themselves. And finally, the motives must be just. As contradictory as it may seem, violence can be used to restore peace by resisting evil bent on destroying peace.

All of this is simple and straightforward to rational, objective minds—that is, to minds unlike most of ours. It is difficult for us normal people to sort out our motives. We disagree about what is evil, and about when violence is needed. We have all let our anger get the best of us before. How do we fallible creatures make the decision to use violent means in the service of justice and peace?

It Takes One to Know One

Our aversion to hypocrisy paints us into a moral corner. Just ask baby boomer parents who made all the wrong choices about sex and drugs how they feel about setting very different rules for their own children. Many boomer parents report feeling very uneasy about warning their own kids away from behaviors that they happily indulged in when they were young, but which they now regret. They feel like hypocrites.

This phenomenon reminds me of childhood name-calling. If someone called you a geek or a sissy, you dropped the hypocrisy bomb: "It takes one to know one!" If you had even the slightest hint of the shortcoming you were noticing in someone else, you had no right to say anything, no room to talk. If you did open your mouth, you were guilty of hypocrisy, what seems today to rank as the only unforgivable sin.

Jesus spoke about judging and responding to evil in this oft-quoted passage: "Why do you see the speck in your neighbor's eye, but do not notice the log in your own eye?" (Matthew 7:3). Some say that you have no right to criticize or judge others unless your own house is completely in order. Jesus' words seem to imply that we should attend to our own moral shortcomings until we have completely eradicated them. Only when we have achieved undiluted righteousness do we have the moral standing to take anyone else to task. But let's face it, we will never be perfectly virtuous. If we were to follow this interpretation of Jesus' teaching, we could never judge evil as evil. And if we lacked the capacity to name evil, we certainly could not respond to it in any meaningful sense.

But this interpretation is off the mark. Encouraging us to lead lives of self-absorption is not at all in keeping with Jesus' life or his teachings; the interpretation I've outlined above would lead to endless moral navel-gazing. We would spend all of our time reflecting on the state of our own souls, ferreting out our character defects, and pursuing programs devoted to our own self-improvement. Even though we would ostensibly be pursuing righteousness, in the end, our lives would have been devoted to ourselves: the pursuit of the self-justified me.

Jesus taught us that we are completely incapable of justifying our own existence; he came to justify us. As he said, "For the Son of Man came not to be served but to serve, and to give his life a ransom for many" (Mark 10:45). You do not remove the log from your own eye and then receive the moral authority to judge others as less moral than you are. Instead, you see your own need for mercy and gratefully recognize that you have received that mercy. You can recognize evil because you know it from the inside; you have been held captive by it, and been ransomed from its grip.

Christians do not approach evil with smug self-righteousness or condescension. Instead, we remember the dreadful effects of evil upon our own lives, and compassionately look on those who are swept up in evil's destructive power. It is our duty to restrict evil's territory, as it were, and to liberate those oppressed by its dehumanizing rule. We do not sit by idly, watching slavery, racism, and genocide. The liberation by violent means of Nazi death camps was an act of moral heroism.

My point here is not to assume a posture of moral superiority over others, nor to assume that whichever virtue we embody gives us permission to condescend or to think of someone else as beyond redemption. Part of what we find so soul-stretching about Jesus is his capacity to extend mercy even to slave holders, racists, and ethnic cleansers. We are not self-righteous; we know ourselves to be under the reign of the only true, good, and just King. We are dedicated to extending his reign and liberating even those who have committed hideous, destructive acts. We stand for good against evil because Jesus Christ ransomed us from that very evil. We have received mercy. Our goal is not to destroy evil but to extend the reign of the merciful King, Jesus Christ.

I have been hinting here at a more cosmic dimension of good and evil. Christians live under the reign of Christ. Evil characterizes an alternative kingdom. Our struggle with good and evil relates to the human will, but it also involves much more than that. It is to this topic that I now turn.

The Lion, the Lamb, and the War to End All Wars

"The war to end all wars" was a popular phrase used to describe World War I. Woodrow Wilson used it in his speech to Congress in 1917 in which he called America to arms. In Wilson's view, America would not be entering the war merely to defeat a human enemy or rival nation state, but to "vindicate principles of peace and justice in the life of the world as against selfish and autocratic power." Wilson believed that the world order and the status of human beings in that order were at stake. His dream was to establish a just and peaceful order that would prevent the kind of violence seen on European battlefields. As we know, not two decades later, Europe again erupted in an orgy of violence with the rise of Nazism. Conflicts of various scope and in various parts of the world have raged ever since. War, it seems, simply refuses to die.

Christians believe that Wilson was right to see that every war has underlying principles more powerful than passing national interests and political advantage. Some believe that his vision to end all war was flawed only by his use of force. They insist the lesson to be learned is that war can never be ended by war; only pacifist commitment will end it. Scripture leads us to draw a different conclusion. Even in just wars, final victory is not attainable; no human action could eradicate evil, as such. This is because we do not wage war against humans alone. Satan, evil personified, wages war against us. In the face of one loss, evil regroups and presses on to a new front. The apostle Paul put it this way: "For our struggle is not against flesh and blood, but against the rulers, against the authorities, against the powers of this dark world and against the spiritual forces of evil in the heavenly realms" (Ephesians 6:12).

War is a clear example of the recurring appearance of the force that brings human misery, but there are other vivid examples. The United States, for instance, made a clear moral advancement by abolishing slavery in 1865. However, now human trafficking simply takes new forms; young and powerless people are pressed into sexual slavery.

Nothing less than the very order of things is at stake in our struggle against evil. There are, to paraphrase Paul, spiritual forces that resist and rebel against God's reign of perfect justice and perfect peace. Human individuals and human choices are certainly involved, but so too are relentless forces beyond human control. Christians do not believe that God and Satan are equally mighty beings in an eternal struggle for dominance. That is a religion called Manichaeism, which we long ago rejected. Evil is a part of the creation, distorted and deformed nearly beyond recognition. Satan and those wittingly or unwittingly in league with him distort and deform themselves by striving for an alternative vision of the basic order of creation, a vision that always involves oppression, violence, fear and degradation. Christ decisively won the battle with evil on the cross, but now, before he ascends to his throne and eradicates all evil once and for all, Satan is going through his death throes. This is the theme of the Book of Revelation.

In the time between Christ's death and resurrection and his second coming, evil is throwing its final temper tantrum, as it were. Carolyn Arends illustrates this in a striking way in her article "Satan's a Goner," published in *Christianity Today*. She likens the evil we experience to the tortured spasms of a beheaded giant snake she once saw in the home of some missionaries. Though it was dead, the snake's decapitated body thrashed about for hours, and destroyed much of the contents of the home. So it is with Satan after the cross. He's a goner, but he's making a terrible mess until he realizes it. In the second coming, Jesus will end this rebellious destruction once and for all. Our ongoing struggle with evil is neither hopeless nor fruitless. But our hope lies in Jesus' final triumph, not in our merely mortal strategies and human strength.

The nature of Jesus' final triumph tells us everything about the struggle of good and evil, and how God shall win in the end. Consider this passage from Revelation:

> Then I saw in the right hand of him who sat on the throne a scroll with writing on both sides and sealed with seven seals. And I saw a mighty angel proclaiming in a loud voice, "Who is worthy to break the seals and open the scroll?" But no one in heaven or on earth or under the earth could open the scroll or even look inside it. I wept and wept because no one was found who was worthy to open the scroll or look inside. Then one of the elders said to me, "Do not weep! See, the Lion of the tribe of Judah, the Root of David, has triumphed. He is able to open the scroll and its seven seals." Then I saw a Lamb, looking as if it had been slain, standing at the center of the throne.
> —Revelation 5:1–6

Jesus is at once the lamb that was slain and the lion that reigns. On the cross, he showed evil its own futility. He suffered all that evil could dish out until it had exhausted itself, only to rise from the dead beyond the touch of all the suffering and death at evil's disposal. When he comes again, he will say the final, decisive no to all who cling to the way of coercion, oppression, and violence. This will be the war to end all wars. The Lamb who is also the Lion shall establish the kingdom of God on earth as it is in heaven. As we read in Revelation:

> I saw the Holy City, the new Jerusalem, coming down out of heaven from God, prepared as a bride beautifully dressed for her husband. And I heard a loud voice from the throne saying, "Look! God's dwelling place is now among the people, and he will dwell with them. They will be his people, and God himself will be with them and be their God. He will wipe every tear from their eyes. There will be no more death or mourning or crying or pain, for the old order of things has passed away."
> —Revelation 21:2–4

In the meantime, we live with wheat and weeds inextricably intertwined. That is why criminal trials like the case of Casey Anthony grab our attention.

Living with the Weeds

For weeks, the news media devoted hours of attention to the ongoing trial of Casey Anthony. This is unsurprising, given the details of the case. Casey Anthony was a young mother charged with the death of her two-year-old daughter, Caylee. People were shocked by the idea that a mother might have killed her child, and they wanted things set right for Caylee somehow. Eventually, Casey was acquitted of the charges against her. When the jury handed down the not-guilty verdict, public obsession turned to outrage in some quarters, while other observers began to criticize our habit of rushing to judgment in such public cases. The Anthony trial underscored for us a spiritual challenge that all followers of a good God must face. People do terrible things to each other every day, and we believe that a good God will set things right somehow. But cases go unsolved. Evils go unaddressed. After a while, many of us ask, "Where is God in this?"

Remember Jesus' parable about the landowner with weeds in his wheat field. Jesus is doing something about it, even though it may not seem that way to most mortal observers because we do not fully understand the weed issue, or its only possible solution (Matthew 13:24–30). The world we inhabit is actually God's kingdom. Certainly, there is more to God's kingdom than what meets the mortal eye; there is earth and there is heaven. But earth is a part of God's kingdom, and heaven is not some place separate from earth. When Matthew uses the phrase, "the kingdom of heaven," he means the sphere in which the sovereign God reigns. God created this planet and the entire universe, including the heavenly realms presently occupied by angels, archangels, and the saints who have gone before us. By all rights, each square inch of the cosmos owes loyalty, devotion, and submission to God. And yet, this grand wheat field has a wicked infestation of weeds.

Earthly gardeners spot weeds and yank them out by the roots. It is strenuous, tedious, seemingly perpetual work, but it can be done. If you do not get to them soon enough, the weeds will choke out the whole garden. Surely God knows this. So what is taking him so long? Why hasn't he already plucked out the wicked weeds so that we stalks of wheat can grow unmolested? As crazy as it sounds—and let me tell you, God is crazy in love with us, to use a phrase by Francis Chan—God is giving us time. He wants us to decide which kingdom we want to inhabit. There are only two: the kingdom of heaven and the kingdom of weeds.

The parable of the weeds teaches us that we are living through a period of insurrection. For a time, God allows for revolt against his rule. His reign is not autonomous; it involves our free will. Therefore, we must have the capacity to say yes or no. God does not permit you to say no forever, though. You may say no, but then you may not remain in his kingdom.

Satan wants a kingdom of weeds, and God will give it to him. It is called hell. Any weed can remain in the kingdom of wheat, so long as the weed will let God make him into wheat. None of us, you see, is wholly wheat or wholly weed. We cannot make ourselves into unadulterated wheat. The atoning sacrifice of Christ on the cross is the decisive difference between weeds and wheat. Christ transforms those who accept that sacrifice from weeds to wheat. He pays the price for our sins and attributes his own perfect righteousness to us.

In the end, weeds cannot remain in the kingdom of heaven as weeds; they will be cast into the kingdom of weeds they apparently long for. There will be a kingdom where mothers cast away children because they are inconvenient, where people get their way through intimidation and bullying, where lying is the rule and not the exception, where bonds of affection last only as long as they benefit people, where fidelity is a joke, and where an individual's wants take precedence over all other considerations. That is hell. If you want it, you may have it. God gives us the time we need to see if that really is what we want. The apostle Peter put it this way: "The Lord is not slow to fulfill his promise as some count slowness, but is patient toward you, not wishing that any should perish, but that all should reach repentance" (2 Peter 3:9). God is connecting the dots at a pace in keeping with his gracious design.

For some, the very suggestion that God would condemn anyone to hell is both emotionally shocking and intellectually unacceptable. They cannot reconcile the idea of a loving God with eternal torment. In the following chapter, we will explore the subject of hell. God made us in his image, so all of human life has an eternal trajectory. The infinitely loving God does allow for hell, but in a way that seems at once surprising and familiar.

Chapter Five

Picturing Eternity: Heaven and Hell

Eventually, we all face our own mortality. The fact that our time on this earth is limited gives rise to a question: will this have all been worth it? Will all my struggles and heartaches and joys and triumphs amount to anything? Will the relentless passage of time simply erase my sweet and tender moments with my wife and my children? The Bible tells us that we are created in the image of God (Genesis 1:26–27). This means, among other things, that we can and do yearn for eternal things. We want our lives to matter, beyond today or next month or even the memories of our children and grandchildren. We want assurance that our lives will amount to more than anonymous dust scattered among the stars. Even the most famous author, rock star, religious leader, political figure, military hero, or moral teacher will be utterly forgotten by humans in a million years. To the cosmos, a million years is a mere nanosecond. If we will eventually be utterly forgotten, then surely none of this is worth it. What is the point? What justifies our existence for eternity?

Christians believe that the crucified and risen Christ justifies our existence. Through him, God connects the dots of our lives into an eternal picture. This life is fleeting, but we believe that it is but a foretaste of a greater life that Jesus came to offer us. There is a life after this life, an eternal life in which all the dots of our lives are connected. A hope-inspired life is one sustained and empowered by the promise that God will complete the picture that we now see only partially. Despite our perceived failures, anonymity, or unimportance, the lives we live will be an indispensable part of God's plan. God will redeem our sorrows and our losses, even our sinful choices and our indifference. Trials that looked as though they would break our hearts forever and leave us in shambles will be precisely the points when God's resurrection power gave us the new life that only he can offer. Strictly speaking, Christians await the second coming of Christ to renew heaven and earth. But with the risk of confusion, many people talk about this as going to heaven.

If we could stop right here, everyone would be perfectly happy. Unfortunately, this is not where Christian teaching ends. We also believe that life can be utterly unjustified. That is what we mean by hell; the dots remain unconnected and it is all eternally futile. There is no greater agony than the torture of this futility. Scripture teaches us that God condemns some to eternal torment. This really disturbs contemporary minds. As Rob Bell famously asked, would a loving God send millions of people, or even one person, to eternal torment? In our multicultural world, debate about hell becomes especially heated when Christians insist that eternal life comes only through Jesus Christ.

The Holy Scriptures teach us that God does, in fact, love us, and that he sets things right. Heaven and hell play a role in God's response to his fragile, fractured creation. In Scripture and throughout church tradition, there is solid teaching about our eternal destiny. Yet what Jesus taught about the role of heaven and hell has been debated, misunderstood, and misrepresented for centuries. Before examining what Scripture actually teaches about heaven and hell, we should correct a common misconception. Then the field will be clear to discuss how a loving God could send someone to hell, and what eternal life with Christ is like.

The Paradise Ticket Narrative

Many Christians teach, preach, and believe that eternal life is like getting your parking ticket validated so that you can pass into paradise. Let's call this approach to eternal life the Paradise Ticket Narrative. According to this narrative, the hope of an afterlife boils down to getting into paradise, which is what many people call heaven. Paradise, or heaven, is a like a really great, eternal vacation spot. There is no suffering, no sorrow, no hunger, no violence—just peace and joy. Now don't get me wrong, in Jesus Christ, God does promise us eternal life, and it does looks something like this description. But the Paradise Ticket Narrative misses the main ingredient.

You could want to go to a really nice place, wanting eternal comfort, fun, and entertainment, without caring whether God were there or not. In other words, your chief concern in life could simply be the quality of your own life on an eternal scale. In the Paradise Ticket Narrative, God is little more than a gatekeeper. His role is to make sure that your ticket to paradise is valid, and to put it frankly, once you get in, you couldn't care less whether God shows up or not, as long as he keeps the place tidy and ensures that you have a paradise-worthy experience.

The only question about salvation, then, is how to validate your ticket. There are two ways: faith and works. Some people say that you have to think right, that God admits only those with the right concepts of God and of his Son. Others insist that only righteous personal conduct validates that ticket to paradise; your concepts of God and Jesus do not really matter, as long as you are merciful and compassionate. Some people mistakenly believe that when Paul spoke of salvation by faith alone, he meant having the right theology. Another group of people read the letter to James, and thinking that faith without works is dead, they insist that works of mercy open the gates of heaven to people of every faith and even to those with no faith at all.

So, at the end of our lives, God checks your ticket. Depending upon your specific theology, he will look either for a faith stamp or a works stamp. If he sees the proper stamp, he grants you admission to heaven. If your ticket lacks the proper validating stamp, he sends you to hell. Now, if we truly believed God to be an indifferent turnstile operator, we might not balk. But Christians insist that God is loving, above all else. This is precisely why so many people struggle with the idea that God could condemn anyone to hell.

Let's switch metaphors for moment. Genuine love is not a reward for our achievements; it is a freely given gift. Many people see heaven and hell as reward and punishment. God measures us according to a moral or theological standard, then dispenses judgment. Those who measure up go to heaven, and the misfits and slackers go to hell. In this model of heaven and hell, God acts solely as an objective judge. We spend our lives scrambling to build an adequate moral resume.

Life and the afterlife, in this model, are all about measuring up. If we believe God is loving, then in this model, God must become an infinitely lenient grader. Love requires that he completely eliminate failing grades. Everyone passes, gets promoted, and wins a trophy at the end of the celestial season.

To return to our original metaphor, God checks to make sure that every ticket is validated. But he is a kindly ticket taker. Out of the goodness of his heart, he does not want anyone to miss the show in paradise. So, with a wink and a nod, in this model, he lets everyone through the turnstiles. Any other response would be unloving, exclusionary, and judgmental. Love, after all, is unconditional acceptance.

In the final analysis, God's judgment will never be reconciled with his loving character as long as we work within the framework of the Paradise Ticket Narrative, and fortunately for us, this is not what the Bible teaches. We need to set this narrative aside and start anew with a more accurate understanding of God's relationship with his creation. Only then will heaven and hell begin to make sense as part of the infinitely loving God's redemption of his fallen creation.

Let's start with God's reason for creating everything from nothing in the first place. The Paradise Ticket Narrative assumes that we are in this life to enjoy ourselves. We seek to win God's approval and acceptance so that we can keep enjoying ourselves for eternity. In contrast, the Bible teaches us that God created everything because he is good and loving. "The Lord is good to all; his mercy is over all that he has made" (Psalm 145:9). In other words, we exist because God's love brought us into being. In his love, God wills for us the greatest joy, which consists of knowing the love that God has for us, and of returning that love to him with all of our hearts, minds, souls, and strength. As Paul said, "He predestined us for adoption as sons through Jesus Christ, according to the purpose of his will, to the praise of his glorious grace, with which he has blessed us in the Beloved" (Ephesians 1:5–6).

From the very start, God chose to involve himself in a big gamble. Love is freely given; it cannot be coerced. The ability to love carries with it the capacity to withhold love. When God created us to be loving beings, he knew that we could choose to reject his love for us or to withhold our love from others, to refuse the very love that makes our lives worth living. If we are to be truly free, hell must be at least a logical possibility for us. This is the root of eternal damnation, just as accepting love freely offered is the foundation of heaven. God leaves us free to choose hell.

Choosing Hell

It seems improbable that anyone would freely choose hell instead of heaven. A choice like this would be obviously self-destructive. No one, you might think, would willingly choose eternal agony. And yet, that is precisely what the Scriptures teach. We do not choose hell in a single decision; there is no identifiable eternal destiny election day, no voting booth with heaven and hell as competing candidates. Instead, we make the choice by developing spiritual habits which have an eternal trajectory.

God made us in his image (Genesis 1:26–27). This means that our spiritual lives go on into eternity. Our bodies will die and decompose, but our souls will continue, awaiting the final resurrection and the gift of what Paul called a spiritual body (1 Corinthians 15:44). Your interior life of thinking, feeling, willing, and desiring is the dimension of yourself that will endure after death. That is your spiritual life, and it is a life that you form over time. We develop habits of thinking and feeling and desiring that we carry with us into life after life. The habits we form suit us for eternal citizenship. Depending upon the sorts of habits we form, we prepare ourselves for residency in either heaven or hell.

Before all this starts sounding like a flight of imagination, let's turn to Jesus' teaching itself. "For what does it profit a man to gain the whole world and forfeit his soul?" (Mark 8:36). Jesus means, "You can't take it with you." he shows us the deeper spiritual truth embedded in the phrase. It is not just stuff that you can't take with you. Depending on how you live in this life, you could lose your soul. Let me explain.

The soul is that part of us that endures the death of the body. When you die, your soul departs the body and waits in the nearer presence of our Lord for the final resurrection, the new heaven, and the new earth. God promises to give us new spiritual bodies (1 Corinthians 15:44). The soul is your identity. It is who you are. And you form your identity, your soul, by worshipping. Whatever you devote yourself to as your highest good determines who you are; it shapes your soul. If you let some finite thing, anything less than God, define you, you will lose your soul. You can't take it with you. You will become a nobody.

Let's use one of Jesus' own parables to illustrate this: the story of Lazarus and the rich man. There once was an abjectly poor man named Lazarus, and a rich man who wore fine clothes and regularly enjoyed great feasts. Dressed in filthy rags, starving and sick, Lazarus huddled in a corner on the rich man's porch. The rich man walked right past him every day. Then Lazarus and the rich man died. Lazarus went to heaven and the rich man went to hell. From heaven, Abraham spoke to the rich man in hell, telling him that he had already received his reward in the world (Luke 16:19–31). Notice two specific details about life after this life for the rich man: He had already received his reward in this world, and he was not named.

Abraham meant that the rich man had worshipped the finite things of this world. In all likelihood, the rich man did not realize he was worshipping material wealth and earthly status. He was probably a practicing Jew. He kept the law, attended synagogue, and offered the prescribed sacrifices at the temple. But what he really worshipped, what he counted on to connect the dots of his life, were his material comforts and his status.

We do not actively choose our highest good at each moment. Rather, we gradually accumulate a habit relying upon something to connect the dots of our lives. Worship is not just what we do on Sunday mornings; it is our acknowledgement of something as our highest good by patterning our lives in a way that serves that highest good. Take a look at the rich man's habits. As far as we can tell, he spent his days so obsessed with his appearance and what he would consume that he could step right over another man suffering in his doorway. His soul was shaped by the pursuit of his own comfort and by his indifference to others. In the depths of hell, He never once asked God, "Get me out of here!" Instead, he said, "Send Lazarus to dip the tip of his finger in water and cool my tongue; for I am in agony in these flames." The rich man did not want to escape hell. He preferred to raise his comfort level from agony to misery, and still could only see Lazarus as an instrument for his own relief. It never seemed to cross his mind that his pursuit of comfort, his self-absorption, and his lack of compassion made him at home in hell.

This is why the man has no name. The things he worshipped shaped his identity. He spent his whole life building an "empire of dirt," to borrow a lyric from the Nine Inch Nails song "Hurt." He couldn't take it with him. More importantly, he could not take that identity with him beyond the grave. To quote a John Ortberg title, *When the Game Is Over, It All Goes Back in the Box*. All the things and all the status he had accumulated, and with which he had identified himself, passed away with his body. Without them, he was nobody. He couldn't take his worldly identity with him into the afterlife because he had to leave behind everything that he had used to give himself an identity. He had gained the whole world and lost his soul.

Most of us know what it is like to involve ourselves in activities which slowly become habits that diminish the quality of our lives. They seem like a good idea at the time. Alcoholics and drug addicts report almost universally that the early days of their substance use felt terrific. They were not afraid of people. They could carry on lively conversations at parties. Their cares seemed to disappear. Only later did they experience the destruction of their relationships, finance, health, and reputations.

We get into spiritual habits before we know it, and some of them eventually make us miserable. It feels great to judge others until we realize that we will not be happy with anybody, including ourselves, as long as we spend our time finding fault. Shopping works to boost our sagging feelings until we start to realize how empty that full closet makes us feel. Name your own poison.

The Hebrews wandered in the wilderness for forty years after escaping Egypt. It should have taken them only three weeks to get to the Promised Land. But geographical relocation was not the central point of the journey from the Red Sea to what would become Israel. The Hebrews needed time to become the people of God. They needed time to develop a new way of thinking, feeling, and willing toward their God, and toward each other.

God's plan was that, over time, their souls would begin to form a habit of making the God of Abraham, Isaac, and Jacob their highest good. They were preparing themselves to be a people who relied upon God's promise to connect the dots of their lives. Only in this way could they be genuinely at home in the Promised Land. Therefore, the exodus was not principally about geographical relocation; it was about spiritual transformation. For the most part, such transformation happens gradually. We form habits, especially the habit of organizing our daily lives around one highest good. The habit of worship has an eternal trajectory. It is important to be clear here. The key teaching of the Christian faith is not an admonition to form virtuous habits in order to win God's favor. Rather, the Christian good news is that Jesus saves us from our various forays into idolatry, that is, into worshipping something less than God.

Now imagine what it might have happened if the rich man in the parable of Lazarus and the rich man had responded differently when he found himself in hell. In the parable, he only wanted a more comfortable hell. Imagine instead that he had said to Jesus, "I don't want to be here. Please get me out!" But then, we must remember the Apostles' Creed. Jesus reaches out to us where we are to make us into the people he dreams we can be, but his strategy to help us does not amount to helping us escape. Instead, he comes to join us. That changes everything, including us.

Heaven Comes to Earth: There Goes the Neighborhood

Years ago, I participated in Kairos Prison Ministry. Several participants would bring guitars into the prison to play music for the inmates during worship. The inmates' favorite song was the hymn "I'll Fly Away." I'm not making this up. The inmates especially liked the line, "Like a bird from prison bars has flown, I'll fly away." "I'll Fly Away" is actually about going to heaven; it is right there in the first line: "Some glad morning when this life is o'er, I'll fly away."

Lots of people think about heaven exactly this way, as someplace you go after this life is over. They think we leave this world for a different place which is infinitely better. Most people do not get into the details of the plumbing in the new place, but they do know that it is better. And did we mention that it is someplace other than here? There are, however, entrance requirements: living a good life, repenting your sins, believing in Jesus. Get these on your resume!

The problem is that it this is not what the Bible actually says. The apostle John said, "I saw the holy city, the new Jerusalem, coming down out of heaven from God" (Revelation 21:2). Souls do not flying away from planet earth up to heaven. The New Jerusalem descends to earth. "See, the home of God is among mortals. He will dwell with them; they will be his peoples, and God himself will be with them" (Revelation 21:3). God comes to dwell with his people, right here, where we are, on our block, maybe even next door. There goes the neighborhood!

Those of us who own homes know that the character of the neighbors influences the quality of the neighborhood. When Joy and I lived in Jacksonville, Florida, some new neighbors moved into the house across the street. We saw them ride up on a Harley, and didn't think much of it, initially, but when all of their friends rode up on Harleys at midnight and started playing music so loudly our windows vibrated, we started to get a little nervous. Their drunken confrontation with the police at 3:00 a.m. did not help much either. We imagined the house across the street eventually deteriorating, other neighbors short-selling to escape violence and crime, our whole street occupied, one house at a time, by a biker gang. There goes the neighborhood!

As it turns out, God's salvation plan for his creation involves relocation. He will not transport our individual souls to some distant plane, however; he will move into our neighborhood. And the neighborhood will never be the same after he does. In the Lord's Prayer, we say, "Thy kingdom come, thy will be done, on earth as it is in heaven." We are holding God to his promise. He says he will move into our neighborhood; no one is being forced to move out of the neighborhood. But God's very presence will repel all of the behaviors and attitudes that make people dangerous, uncaring, indifferent, destructive, or self-centered neighbors. Racism, greed, murder, rape, lust, robbery, conceit, war, hatred, and unforgiveness must all vacate the neighborhood.

God wants us to stay in the neighborhood, even if our very souls must be vastly renovated. The departure of some of these destructive and self-destructive character flaws and behaviors may leave big gaps in our souls. Jesus stands ready to repair us to a state that better than we could even imagine. But if we are so attached to any of these distortions of God's creation that we cannot live without them, then we must leave the neighborhood to keep them.

You may not know how to see people who are very different from you as the beloved children of God, but Jesus can change that, if you let him. You may not be able to imagine a life in which you seek another's welfare before considering your own comfort or status, but Jesus can. Jesus wants you in the neighborhood, but he will not settle for a neighborhood that feels anything like hell. If that is the sort of neighborhood you want, God's neighborhood is not the place for you.

Jesus will not whisk us away from earth. Instead, he will come again to renew both heaven and earth. This question still remains, for non-Christians and Christians alike: What happens to people who do not believe in Jesus?

Who Does Jesus Save?

It is hard for many of us to reconcile the idea of a loving God with the doctrine that he could condemn millions of people to eternal torment in hell. Mind you, we also want justice. God should hold Hitler, Stalin, and Pol Pot accountable for their actions. That goes for unrepentant rapists and murderers, too. But do you have to believe in Jesus to avoid eternal punishment? I mean, what about good people like Gandhi? He was a Hindu. Non-Christian children died in the devastating earthquake and tsunami that occurred recently in Japan. Will they spend eternity devoured by flames because they were taught the wrong religious beliefs?

Let me start by saying that these questions can be a dodge, or at the very least, they can lead us in the wrong direction for understanding God's mercy and judgment. Remember that Jesus told us not to judge (Matthew 7:1). His teaching is the key to our response to such questions about the eternal destiny of those who do not know Jesus. However, the answer may not be especially satisfying to some.

Jesus taught us to live within the limits of our capacity to make moral judgments. We have been given the ability to judge specific actions in a very limited way. We can see that an action adheres to or transgresses against moral law. With difficulty, we can begin to make out patterns of behavior that suggest the outline of a person's enduring character. With less clarity, we can discern extenuating circumstances around an action. Standing on even shakier ground, we can speculate about a person's motives and intentions.

When Jesus told us to withhold judgment, he was reminding us that we do not know as much as we are tempted to believe we know. Our original sin was to eat of the Tree of the Knowledge of Good and Evil. We frequently slip into assuming greater moral authority over and spiritual insight into other people than we genuinely have. Only God has infinite, flawless judgment and insight. To put it simply, it is not our place in life to determine whether or not a person is hell-bound. Conversely, our powers of moral and spiritual discernment are not great enough to determine who should go to heaven. People do bad things. People do good things. We may loathe some people and wish to spend eternity somewhere far away from them. Our affections for other people may make us yearn to be with them forever. None of this amounts to us being able to say with any justification who has chosen hell and who has surrendered to heaven.

We peek at the infinite expanse of the spiritual world through a keyhole. We catch but a partial perspective at best. We cannot see where other people's choices will lead them, or the turning points in their future, or the hidden thoughts of their heart, or how God will use even the smallest opportunity to intervene. Only God can see all of this. We are not privy to Christ's approach to different people in the twilight consciousness on the threshold of this life and the next. But I have been at enough deathbeds to believe that mysterious things happen there.

First and foremost, we should each question ourselves about Jesus and salvation. Can I trust Jesus with my eternal destiny? Once I answer yes, I see that I can entrust Him with the eternal destiny of others. That is as far as I can go. I can even entrust those I care most about to his judgment and mercy.

I learned an important lesson when my then-toddler daughter Meredith underwent open-heart surgery. The possibility that she might die sucked my wife Joy and me into an emotional quicksand. I reached a turning point when I realized that if I could trust Jesus with my life, I could trust him with hers. Let me be clear about this insight: I did not assume that my faith would prevent Meredith from dying on the operating table. Instead, I realized that his love for her, like his love for me, was stronger than death itself. Jesus does not promise to save us from heartbreak. His resurrection promises that life will come even from death, and joy from sorrow.

So then, what about Gandhi and other people who die in ignorance of Christ? What about those who cannot believe, because negative experiences with abusive evangelical parents or predatory Catholic priests? I do not know. But I know Jesus, and I trust him. I know that some readers will say, "How can I trust someone who would condemn these good, innocent people?" My response is that that particular question will lead you to a dead end. It delays the basic question that Jesus asks each of us: Will you trust me? He reaches his hand out to each and every one of us in some way. Each of us can take it or refuse to take it. We can be assured that he reaches out his hand as far as he can, as persistently as he can, and in ways that baffle, astound, and even scandalize us.

Love's Invitation

The question still remains: Do you have to believe in Jesus Christ to go to heaven? Or, to frame it in a slightly different way: Will those who die without faith in Jesus Christ as their Lord and Savior inherit eternal torment in hell? Let's recap some of what I have suggested so far before laying out the answer.

- God created us to love him and to love one another. By design, we yearn for eternal life with God and his children.
- God loves us first. We respond.
- God wants what is best for us: eternal life with him and his children.
- Love requires freedom. We can freely accept God's love, or reject it. We can surrender to heaven, or choose hell.
- We develop spiritual habits of accepting or rejecting God's love in our everyday lives. The habits we develop have an eternal trajectory. They give us a foretaste of heaven or hell.
- Even when we choose hell in our daily lives, God keeps reaching out to us through his son, Jesus Christ.
- In the end, God loves us enough to give us what we want, even if it breaks his heart. He knows when our rejection of him is final.

I ask that you hold off on drawing your conclusion about Jesus' role in salvation until we have heard from Jesus himself. Jesus said to Nicodemus, "Indeed, God did not send the Son into the world to condemn the world, but in order that the world might be saved through him . . . Those who believe in him are not condemned; but those who do not believe are condemned already, because they have not believed in the name of the only Son of God" (John 3:16–17). Just before his passion, Jesus said to his disciples, "I am the way, and the truth, and the life. No one comes to the Father except through me. If you know me, you will know my Father also. From now on you do know him and have seen him" (John 14: 6–7). Jesus came to save us, not to condemn us. And yet, no one comes to the Father except through Jesus.

Many who believe in God equate love with refusal to condemn. Of course God does not condemn us, they say. He is good. He is loving. Love never judges, not even when someone refuses to follow Jesus. Besides, they continue, most people are good, and good people deserve to go to heaven. Nobody is perfect, but many are good enough. Christian Smith coined a phrase to identify this theology in *Soul Searching: The Religious and Spiritual Lives of American Teenagers*: Moral Therapeutic Deism (MTD). It goes something like this. God created us and watches us from a distance. He expects us to be nice to and tolerant of each other. This is the central message of most religions. Happiness and self-esteem are life's highest goals. God only gets involved in this life when we have a problem. In the end, all good people go to heaven.

But there is something crucial missing from MTD. The fact is, we are broken in ways that we cannot fix for ourselves and that make us unfit for heaven. If we lived for eternity just as we are, we would make a hell of it. Rape, war, murder, racism, lust, greed, hunger, poverty, envious rage, and soul-numbing indifference would come right along with us into the afterlife. Heaven would not be worth the price of admission if it were merely more of the same, forever. Living in eternal misery and conflict is hell, not heaven. God did not send his son to assess our acceptability to him; Jesus does not administer admissions tests to see if we have been good enough to get into heaven. He does not come to condemn; he comes to save us from ourselves, for a life we could not construct for ourselves.

Jesus is not just a great teacher or political instigator or moral example. He is God. He is a man. And not a little bit of God or a little bit of man; He is fully God and fully man. As Paul said, "For in him all the fullness of God was pleased to dwell" (Colossians 1:19). Think of Jesus as God reaching out his hand to us in a way that makes it possible for us to actually take hold of it. Much could and should be said about the atoning sacrifice of the cross, about Jesus' victory over sin and death at the empty tomb, and about his second coming. For now, suffice it to say that Jesus is God's love incarnate. To accept or reject him is to accept or reject God's love—and it is only that love can save us (Colossians 1:20).

So what becomes of those good people from different traditions of faith, especially the ones we love? We all know people wounded by the Church who have experienced toxic and hypocritical talk about Jesus. Who could blame a person who was abused sexually by a Catholic priest or mortally shamed by a Protestant preacher for rejecting Christianity? Are those people condemned to hell?

The Savior reached out his hand to me in a way that, despite my own history of hurt and betrayal, I could recognize through the curtain of my cynicism, defensiveness, and fear. He made himself known to me despite my unenviable habits, my shabby choices, my once fawning devotion to what passes for intellectual sophistication, and my arrogance. Jesus issued an invitation to me. For years, I could not see it for what it was. But he kept at it until it became a clear, recognizable invitation to *me*. He had been clear all along; I was the problem.

Because of who he is, has gone to remarkable lengths to get through to me. I could have turned his invitation down, even after I knew it for what it was. But I accepted it, and that has changed everything, over time. According to his invitation, there is yet more to come. I have every reason to believe that he does the same for everyone. He finds a way to issue his invitation to receive the saving love of God himself.

God's Big Love and the World's Rebellion

"God is love." This is not just a foundational principle of the Christian faith. It is also the basic assumption of what you might call American civic spirituality. In other words, the people who say they believe in God but profess no specific faith are likely to say this about God. We Christians are committed to form our thoughts about God based on his self-revelations in the Bible, but the truth is, many of us don't do our biblical homework. Thus, we end up with the vague cultural notion that God is love. He feels deep affection for us. He does not make moral demands on us, except maybe the moral demand not to make moral demands on anybody else. He never judges us. If we are lucky, or good, or talented, he might help us out in a jam, or even give us some swell gifts, but he generally does not get very involved. He means well, but he is largely ineffectual. This God does not give us hope and joy, because we cannot rely on him for much of anything.

Now let's remind ourselves of the *real* God, the only God who can be our Savior. Jesus is the perfect revelation of God. Many people, some Christians among them, seem to think that Jesus negates the Old Testament picture of God. Some heave a sigh of relief for Jesus and say good riddance to the God of the Old Testament. That God is scary; he commands and judges, gets angry and punishes evil, even goes to war. How barbaric! Couldn't we just forget all of that and concentrate on Jesus, meek and mild?

No, we can't, actually. Jesus Hhimself said, "Do not think that I have come to abolish the Law or the Prophets; I have not come to abolish them but to fulfill them" (Matthew 5:17). Jesus fulfills and perfectly clarifies God's character as it has already been revealed in the Old Testament. If you really want to understand God and his love, you have to look at Jesus. But if you really want to understand Jesus, then you cannot toss out what God has shown you of himself in the Old Testament. You have to find Jesus prefigured in the Old Testament.

For instance, the book of Exodus is the story of God rescuing his people from Egyptian bondage. But honestly, look at how he does it. God goes to war with Pharaoh. God is love and God goes to war. This is hard for us to reconcile, but it is the truth. We are going to examine that by looking closely at God's showdown with Pharaoh, but first we need a little background.

Right from the start, God showed himself to be a God of blessing. He brought everything into being, not just to sit back and enjoy it, but to let us know the joy of sharing his life. The highest expression of God's blessing is the gift of life, a life that reflects his life. Human life is the very image of God because we can freely love like God. We can join in intimate relationships like Adam and Eve. He charges us with promoting life by tending his garden of Eden, and he tells us to go forth and multiply, to increase life and love (Genesis 1:1; 2:25).

This is where the spirituality of popular culture ends. For vaguely spiritual but nonreligious people, it makes no sense to say that God is love and that God goes to war. This is because they forget to consider what God's love confronts every morning when he rolls out of the heavenly sack. They just do not take the story of the fall into account. God made the creation to be a place of life, for life, and he made people to be his servants in nurturing and promoting life. But Adam and Eve, with a little help from Satan, wrecked the celestial bus (Genesis 3:1–24). The creation is now infected with forces dead set against God's blessing agenda. In fact, they are bent on death.

The creation is in rebellion against God. The pharaoh of the Exodus story is an especially vivid example of that rebellion. Keep in mind, as we talk about him, that he is just one example of the broader rebellion against God. This particular pharaoh did not remember Joseph. He hated the Israelites. It is bad enough to hate an ethnic group, but this ethnic group happened to figure centrally in God's plan to bless his fallen world. God said to Abraham, "I will make of you a great nation, and I will bless you and make your name great, so that you will be a blessing" (Genesis 12:2). Israel was God's instrument of blessing. Pharaoh was committed to Israel's destruction; he was at war with God's intention to bless. Pharaoh may have thought he was building a viable alternative to God's world, but in point of fact all that he was able to do—all any rebellion against God can do—was become an instrument of death.

Think about Pharaoh's strategies to kill off the Israelites. He ruthlessly imposed "hard service" on them (Exodus 1:14 NSRV). The Hebrew for "hard service" suggests devastating, overwhelming work. His aim was to crush the life out of them with relentless toil. Getting monuments to himself built was just a nice perk. When this failed to work because the Israelites kept multiplying and thriving, he ordered midwives to murder every newborn Hebrew boy. When this failed, he enlisted the whole population of Egypt to drown "Hebrew" babies. Pharaoh used the word "Hebrew" to mean the riffraff, the nobodies (Exodus 1:15–22).

Do you see how this rebellion expanded its reach? Pharaoh's reign of death began as loathing, and grew into full-blown hatred in his heart. Under the guise of promoting order and security in Egypt, Pharaoh translated his personal animus into a state policy dedicated to ethnic cleansing. He seemed to be guarding against the threat of an ethnic group, but at a deeper level, he was committed to wiping out God's blessing. Pharaoh's rebellion grew to oppression and violence and "pulverizing work." He made ordinary life miserable with the intention of promoting mass death by despair. When that failed, Pharaoh tried individual, state-sanctioned murder by midwife. This strategy also failed. Finally, by Pharaoh's edict, the rebellion against God became the work of the entire citizenry. Pharaoh committed the Egyptians to perform commit infanticide. All Egyptians were ordered to drown any Hebrew infant they laid eyes upon.

Pharaoh's actions were insane. But they illustrate how Satan and those who serve him work. Their rebellion seeks to annihilate every last vestige of God's blessing. The Israelites were in terrible peril, and so are we. We, like the Israelites, face a force too powerful to resist on our own. And so, God goes to war with death on their behalf, on our behalf. God employed a series of increasingly forceful tactics and strategies against Pharaoh. His weak servants, the midwives Puah and Shiphrah, thwarted Pharaoh's scheme by refusing to kill the Israelites' baby boys. God raised up Moses to lead his people out of Egypt. He sent plagues, including the plague of the death of the first-born, against Pharaoh. And finally, when Pharaoh pursued the departing Israelites, God drowned Pharaoh's army in the Red Sea

But this was just one great battle in a long and costly war. The greatest cost of all, the cost that eventually put death itself to death, was Jesus Christ, the only Son of God. Jesus is not a casualty, not a victim, in the usual sense of the word. He is love's supreme and paradoxical weapon. Remember that odd thing that Jesus once said: "Do not think that I have come to bring peace to the earth. I have not come to bring peace, but a sword" (Matthew 10:34). He brought the sword to death itself. On the cross, Jesus died to defeat death, your death and my death, the death that we deserve because of our sins. He is not collateral damage. He is God's perfect love in the flesh, come to defeat death once and for all. In Jesus Christ, the God who is love itself wages war against death itself. And when we put our faith in him to connect the dots of our lives, we are more than conquerors. We are heirs of eternal life.

Mercy Wins

People are still talking about Rob Bell's book *Love Wins*. This is a remarkably good thing. While I think many of Bell's arguments are underdeveloped, and I disagree with his apparent sympathies for universalism, I do want to give credit where credit is due. Bell's winsome style is captivating. His pastoral sense of the concerns of spiritual people (as opposed to religious people, whatever that distinction really means) is spot on. We all want to be loved and accepted. We cannot bear the thought that we would be rejected for the flaws and faults that we know we have. We are appalled by the idea that people we love, respect, and admire might be condemned to perdition. We live in a multicultural world and sense correctly that we must find a way to live peaceably and respectfully with people who do not share our religious beliefs. Bell has thousands upon thousands of people talking about the nature of God, eternal life, and justice.

One of the problems I have with the book is Bell's starting point. His distortion of the biblical narrative is analyzed with particular clarity in Mark's Galli's excellent book *God Wins*, which I paraphrase here. About traditional Christian teaching, Bell writes, "God is loving and kind and full of grace and mercy—unless there isn't confession and repentance and salvation in this lifetime, at which point God punishes forever" (Bell, *Love Wins*, 64). I believe that Bell reveals a crucial misguided assumption: God is good—check; God is loving—check; God created everything good. We're doing fine so far, but on the next step, we go off the rails. Bell continues: everything is good because God made it; since God is good and loving and kind, he could not possibly condemn anyone to hell for making mistakes. Bell suggests that historical Christian teaching tells us God put us in the world with a passing grade, heaven-ready as it were, and then stands back, waiting for us to fail so he can send us to hell. But a merciful God would not act like that. Well, Bell is right; a merciful God would not act like that.

But what Bell relates is not the Christian story in the first place. Let's set it straight: the good God created a good creation—check. The creation is fallen and in rebellion against God. Ah, Bell softens this point so much it's hardly visible. The Christian starting point is not that everything is good and that a perfectionist God throws wrathful tantrums about those who make a mess. On the contrary, Scripture teaches that the creation is already separated from God. God responds to the brokenness of the world with judgment for sin we have already committed. That judgment is simultaneously just and merciful. The cross of Christ pays the debt for sin—it is a debt we could not possibly pay ourselves. The cross reconciles us to God and makes us heirs of eternal life. Our part is to accept this freely given gift. Bell probably does not reject the doctrine of the fall, but it certainly does not figure much in his discussion of judgment and mercy. As a result, he obscures how a loving God could also be a God of judgment.

What we are discussing here includes what theologians sometimes call a low doctrine of humanity. I know what some of my readers must be thinking. "You just think people are no good! Well, I'm done with felling guilty! That's why I'm not religious in the first place!" Much teaching that passes for the Gospel instructs us to rid ourselves of unwarranted guilt. God loves us just the way we are because he made us that way. We should love ourselves just as we are. This is only partially true, and incomplete. The good God authored a good creation, but we are now heirs of the fall. We were born into a fallen world with fallen hearts. God loves us before we are love-worthy. That kind of love does not leave us unchanged. It makes us more than we were when God found us. Loving myself the way I am is not the Gospel. The Gospel is knowing through the cross that God loves me as I am, and that this love is changing me.

Let's look at this practically for a moment. Imagine you have done something unkind, said something thoughtless, or nurtured uncharitable thoughts. If you are anything like me, this won't require any imagination at all, just recalling a memory honestly. If we take the approach suggested by Bell (even if he does not explicitly advocate it), then there are two ways to interpret this behavior. We could assert that you are good. This is just human, we might say. The misery you have caused was unintended, or not that bad, or not your problem. The misery you feel is a product of unwarranted guilt, so maybe you need to check in with a counselor. In other words, you wind up indifferent, self-absorbed, and with a lingering sense that things are not as swell as you are telling yourself. Or, we could say that this behavior was indeed bad, but you are still good enough. But that is a concept that will never give you rest: good enough. You will either worry whether you are good enough to avoid condemnation, or you will resign yourself to a tepid life with no hope of unadulterated joy.

The Gospel teaches something radically different. When I acknowledge and repent my sins, I experience elation, not shame, because at that moment, I know a love that even my worst moments could never repulse. I have no need to defend my past failures or selfishness, because they have been redeemed. God is working on me and will never tire of the project. He is connecting the dots of my life in ways I cannot see or comprehend. Through the cross of Jesus Christ, God's judgment looks a lot like mercy to slobs and boneheads like me. The good news is that mercy wins.

CHAPTER SIX

ANGER AND FORGIVENESS: RECONNECTING THE DOTS

We are not meant to be alone. Relationships make our lives worth living (Genesis 2:18). The dots of our lives form a picture because other people matter to us, and because we matter to them. Our personal relationship with Christ ultimately connects the dots of our lives, but following Jesus also means loving other people. We crave belonging, and dread loneliness. And yet, we direct a remarkable amount of energy to erasing the lines that connect us to other people. Of the forces that erase the relational lines of life, anger is one of the most common.

If your contemptuous stares, cutting remarks, lethal coldness, sudden outbursts, or cruel jokes leave everyone in your workplace or family appalled and walking on eggshells, that is anger. It breaks up relationships and dismantles people. Some call anger a deadly sin. Others insist that it is a natural emotion that requires honest, appropriate expression. This is a largely semantic argument that boils down to the kind of question that any Intro Philosophy student knows to ask: What do you mean by anger?

It is safe to assume that we have all experienced something that made our blood pressure rise. This reaction is entirely appropriate in some cases. Cruelty to a child deserves indignation. Disagreements about what movie to watch warrant much less heartburn. The emotion we call anger can arise in the face of injustice, or simply as a result of a bruised ego. Knowing and acknowledging the difference takes some work, maybe a lot of work, for most of us. Let's be clear here: I have no quarrel with perfectly justifiable, appropriately expressed anger. But we all know that it can be awfully difficult to know when we are perfectly justified. It can also be quite a challenge to express powerful emotions of any kind in an appropriate way.

The really striking thing about anger is its ability to hijack us. I am not referring to extreme incidents that make the headlines, like former employees gunning down their office mates, or homicidal road rage. Nor am I talking about those regrettable moments when you impulsively say something or make a gesture or fire off an e-mail that you never would, normally. In angry moments like those, it is as though some raving lunatic has snatched control of your body for an instant and dedicated himself to destroying your most treasured relationships, leaving you with memories that will forever make you cringe. In fact, anger's most effective means of commandeering our souls are far subtler: giving someone the cold shoulder; making a smug, self-righteous Facebook post; thinking that those who differ from us politically or theologically are morons or degenerates.

So what does Jesus have to say about this? "You have heard that it was said to those of ancient times, 'You shall not murder'; and 'whoever murders shall be liable to judgment.' But I say to you that if you are angry with a brother or sister, you will be liable to judgment; and if you insult a brother or sister, you will be liable to the council; and if you say, 'You fool,' you will be liable to the hell of fire" (Matthew 5:21–22). Anger is murder, at least in a manner of speaking. The same habits of thinking and feeling and acting embodied in murder lie on the same continuum as even the most civil expression of anger.

It is not a slippery slope that takes one from everyday resentments and contempt to homicide. At the same time, the distances between contemptuous thoughts to lingering resentments to disparaging gossip to character assassination are shorter than we realize. These lesser angers are radioactive; they must be handled with care. Following the path they pave can poison us. The danger is not any one instance of anger; it is the cumulative effect of feeling, thinking, and acting in certain ways—that is, habit. Over time, we can drift from being occasionally spiteful to being routinely spiteful. We can slowly slide from responding contemptuously to a spouse, child, or friend into a assuming a constantly contemptuous posture. We acquire habits gradually. Habits of the heart and mind form our character, and our actions arise from our character. If we want to change our actions, we rarely find it works to simply say no. Just ask any experienced dieter. Changing a repetitive behavior involves changing deeply ingrained habits. In other words, reforming our behaviors involves character transformation. Unlearning habits and learning new habits is part of what theologians call sanctification. We do not work to replace spiritual habits all on our own; the Holy Spirit works deeply on our souls to rehabilitate us spiritually.

Jesus taught us to develop forgiveness as a spiritual habit. We cannot simply eliminate anger from our emotional vocabulary. However, with Christ's help, we can learn to make forgiveness our definitive spiritual posture. Anger erases the lines connecting the dots between our hearts and others' hearts. In contrast, forgiveness redraws the lines between us and other people. The remarkable thing about Jesus Christ is that he never tells us to stop being angry to gain his affection. Instead, he tells us again and again that he loves us; that is why he wants to help us with our anger. Actually, he has already started helping us with it; it was human anger that nailed him to the cross. He took that anger upon himself, because he knew that it was going to end up killing somebody, and he did not want us to be the victims. he gave us forgiveness to free us not only from our sins but also from the anger that threatens to shatter our relationships.

As our first step in understanding what it means to forgive, and how to go about forgiving in our everyday lives, let's turn to the story of Joseph and his brothers. It highlights anger's destructive effect on relationships, and the power of forgiveness to restore the lines that connect the dots of our hearts.

Learning from Joseph

The Old Testament story of Joseph and his brothers is especially useful in teaching us how to forgive. It warns us not to confuse forgiveness with feeling better, or with the evaporation of our feelings of injury. In fact, part of where we go wrong with forgiveness is equating it with how we *feel* about someone who has wronged us. Forgiveness is what we do (or do not do) based on what we think and what we know with our minds, even in spite of how we feel. Let's review the story and then return to its lessons.

Joseph was Jacob's favorite son, and his brothers resented him for it. After their father had gone out one day, Joseph's brothers sold him into slavery, then convinced father Jacob that wild animals killed his favorite boy. The slave traders took Joseph to Egypt. Through a series of ups and down, Joseph eventually rose to be the second most powerful person in Egypt.

After Joseph's ascent to power, his brothers showed up. There was a famine in the whole region, and the brothers had heard that Egypt had wisely stored away grain for just such an occasion. They had no clue that the powerful official whom they must now beg for grain was their brother. They assumed that by now, he would be dead.

After yanking his brothers' chains, Joseph finally revealed himself to them. They could hardly believe their eyes and ears, and their bad luck. "Oh, no!" they thought. The brother they had tried to kill was now powerful enough to hang them all by their thumbs for the rest of their miserable lives. But Joseph shocked them. He forgave them.

Listen closely to what Joseph told his brothers: "And now do not be distressed or angry with yourselves because you sold me here, for God sent me before you to preserve life . . . So it was not you who sent me here, but God" (Genesis 45:5; 8). He said the same thing, perhaps more clearly, just after his father Jacob died. "As for you, you meant evil against me, but God meant it for good, to bring it about that many people should be kept alive, as they are today" (Genesis 50:20).

What did Joseph say to convince them that they had nothing to fear from him? He did not say, "No hard feelings. That's okay." Nor did he say, "I'm so over that. I've grown so spiritually mature that I can simply rise above such things." He had not, in fact, emotionally healed from the trauma of his youth at all. Before his brothers came, Joseph would cry out so loudly in emotional pain that the servants could hear him from behind closed doors. Joseph clearly acknowledged his brothers' malicious intentions and the injuries they caused him. But then Joseph showed us the key to forgiveness: the Sovereign God made something out of Joseph's suffering.

Joseph could have focused on his feelings of injury. He could have focused on the hate his brothers felt for him. He could have focused on their wicked actions. But then, he would have had to find a solution to all these issues, to heal his pains by visiting them on the very ones who wounded him. He could have tortured and killed his brothers with impunity. Where would that have gotten him? It might have given him a brief sense of retribution, but his broken heart would still have been broken. He would still have had all the old memories, wounds, and emptiness of being unloved by his family.

Joseph found a better way: he directs his actions not by how he felt about his brothers, but by what he knew about God. The all-powerful God had made Joseph's suffering crucial not only to Joseph's own life, but also to all the lives of his father's tribe, to the life of Israel, and to the life of the known world. Joseph saved his brothers from starvation rather than killing them because of his knowledge of what the sovereign God had done. God made that suffering the means of new life. Doesn't that story sound familiar?

Jesus suffered and died on the cross. He paid for our sins, and God vindicated that suffering by raising him from the dead. He raised Jesus from the dead so that we could have new life, an eternal life that we can catch a glimpse of even today. Joseph's life foreshadowed what God was to do through his Son, Jesus, for all of us. Jesus suffered to save us from sin and death, just as Joseph suffered to save his people from famine. Jesus gave us a new life through suffering, which was caused by our sins. More than that, he vindicates our suffering. The power of the cross turns our suffering, caused by our own sins and by those of others, into the birth pangs of new life.

This new life is not yet shielded from suffering, but one day, when our time on this planet is over, suffering and even death will be no more. I am sad to say that in this life, people will hurt us, sometimes intentionally and unrepentantly. But as Christians, we will know that Jesus himself is doing something with our suffering. This is the key to following Jesus' command to forgive. Just like Joseph, we can use our minds; we can remember what we know about God.

God does not make us suffer. He promises to do something with our suffering. Forgiveness is not just about making our suffering go away. Jesus instructs us to forgive those who have injured us so that he can make our suffering count for something. In the cross of Christ, our suffering can be the means of holy healing for others. Those who have been rejected will be able to understand how to love unconditionally, and be a balm to the lonely. Those who have gone without material comforts can become God's instrument for generosity. I never cease to be amazed that a man like me, who struggled his entire childhood with a speech impediment, was made an instrument to proclaim the Gospel from a pulpit.

Here is what we already know: we cannot control our feelings, nor can we heal ourselves of misery, sorrow, or suffering. If we make "feeling better" the goal of our lives, we might get temporary relief, but the very thing that upsets us will come back again, sometimes with even greater force.

Jesus teaches us to give our suffering to God, and to do as he commands: show mercy. When we show mercy, he makes our suffering the birthplace of new life. When we trust God to connect the dots, we show mercy. And in the mix, we are likely to grow in an atmosphere of tranquility, love, and joy which we could never achieve if we pursued them as our chief goals.

Forgive-Me-Nots

Forgiveness transforms our lives and restores our broken relationships, but it is still a tall order. Wading through life gives us all plenty of opportunities to forgive others and to need that same forgiveness for ourselves. Yet even with all this practice, we routinely have trouble getting this forgiveness business right. More people come to me for help with forgiving someone who injured them than for any other pastoral issue.

We should not forgive each other merely because the rules say that we should. Indeed, the Bible does not provide a clear-cut, step-by-step process for how to forgive. Jesus taught us to approach life as people who have fouled things up, and who know the joy and relief of God's extravagant mercy. Notice that I am asserting Jesus taught us that we are recipients of unmerited mercy. I am not suggesting that all Christians have gotten their minds around it. Some people say, "I know that God forgives me, but I can't forgive myself." More people than I'd like to count have said this to me. Parents regret being unkind to their children, or regret being absent. People are burdened with persistent remorse for moments of cowardice, intimate betrayals, petty dishonesties, marital infidelities, and a thousand other kinds of personal failings.

Guilt gets bad press these days, but it is actually a healthy response to our own wrongdoing. A well-formed conscience alerts us with pangs of regret when we do something wrong. Feeling sorry for what we have done leads us to admit that we blew it, we were wrong. So far, so good. It is the next step that burdens so many lives. One misstep is to turn guilt about a specific act into a generalized sense of shame. For instance, years after his father committed suicide, Frederick Buechner found a note his father had written tucked inside one of his books. The note read, "I'm no damn good." Buechner's father had given up on himself. People we rub elbows with every day may not take their own lives, but they give up on themselves in small ways. They hide what they think is ugly about themselves for fear of rejection or ridicule.

There is another misstep which may, at first, sound healthy and positive. Some people admit their mistakes and then dedicate themselves to making up for their failings. The problem with this strategy is that it commits us to justifying our own existence. Even if we can make up for the harm we have caused others in the past, it is impossible to guarantee we will live up to our best selves every hour of every day, and thus, never again hurt anyone. Trying to make up for our past is like continuing to borrow in order to get out of debt. We will never catch up. As long as we try to justify our own existence, we will face the same question every day: What have you done for me lately? Today could be the day we find out that what we have done will never be enough.

Forgiveness begins with each one of us. I don't mean that I take the initiative by forgiving others, or that I forgive myself. I mean that forgiveness begins with my sober recognition that I have failed to get things right. I cannot and do not justify my own existence; I am in desperate need of mercy. And Christians believe that this is precisely what we have received. The cross of Jesus Christ has justified our lives once and for all. Entering each day as a recipient of mercy changes everything. Our lives and our responses to others become a response to the inexhaustibly merciful God. So how do we forgive? And does forgiving mean forgetting?

It's Not Okay

Beverly loved children and kittens. She had a fondness for sweets, and routinely overspent on gifts for Christmas and birthdays. Meals were an occasion for her to lavish affection on her family and friends in the form of rich comfort food. These were her character traits, and the reason why her bitter rants caught me off guard. More than a decade after her divorce, any reminder of Beverly's ex-husband sent her into an enraged litany of his cruelties and vices. If I mentioned trying to forgive the man, she gave the same response: "I can forgive, but I can't forget."

In truth, there was a lot for her to forgive. Beverly's ex-husband beat her constantly, threatened her with a gun, and flagrantly cheated on her. Typical of abusers, he isolated her and controlled every aspect of her life. Beverly endured this brutality for fourteen years before finally fleeing with her only child. We can learn a lot about forgiveness from Beverly. The first lesson is the most important, and may be the most difficult for some of us to accept.

Forgiveness is a response to moral wrongdoing. Beverly's ex-husband physically abused her and committed adultery. His actions injured her in body, mind, and soul. Her outrage was entirely appropriate. This outrage is what moral theologians call righteous indignation. Her first step toward forgiveness was to deal with her moral outrage by leaving rather than hiring a hit man. I said that this first lesson might be the most difficult. We live in an age that mistrusts or simply rejects the idea of moral absolutes. Forgiveness can only begin with the starkest realism. There can be no sweeping under the rug or excuse-making. We must name a moral offense for what it is. Without an objective standard by which to measure virtue and vice, it is impossible to take the first step toward forgiveness. I can say that I am hurt or offended, but these are not moral categories. We must acknowledge an objective moral law.

A physician hurts me when he gives me a shot, but he does not need my forgiveness. Your opinion about the current president or one of his predecessors may very well offend me, but again, you do not need my forgiveness. I simply need to get over myself and allow for our difference of opinion. In contrast, consider violence against the innocent, or adultery. These behaviors are more than painful, and they are more than merely offensive; they are sins. Harming the innocent and committing adultery violate an objective moral law.

Now that I have mentioned sin, I have to make another thing clear. Beverly's forgiveness of her ex-husband did not absolve him of his sin. Only God can do this. Absolving sin is what the cross is about. By forgiving her ex-husband, Beverly refused to retaliate. Sometimes we hesitate to forgive because we believe that this absolves the offender of all accountability for his or her behavior. Nothing could be further from the truth. Forgiveness begins with the acknowledgement that a person has done something wrong and that he or she is accountable for it. There is a debt, and the debt has to be paid. Jesus teaches us that his disciples refuse to go into the moral debt-collection business. God is the judge and redeemer of humankind.

There are several more lessons to be learned from Beverly's experience. Does forgiveness heal our hurts? Do we have to get along with people who have hurt us? Why do I keep getting angry about the very thing I have forgiven? Will I ever forget?

Forgiving Again . . . And Again

A friend of mine is a recovering alcoholic. He has been sober for nearly three decades. Much of what he has told me about his journey toward sobriety helps me to understand the spiritual life in general, and to understand forgiveness in particular. My friend said to me, "I had no problem with stopping drinking. I just couldn't stay stopped." In the early days of recovery, my friend would stop drinking for a period of time, and then relapse. The lengths of time he spent on the wagon varied. Sometimes it was only days. A few times, it was months. Then, he would drink again. He could not stay stopped. Now he is sober, one day at a time. He has been sober for nearly thirty years' worth of todays, but he always remembers that today's spiritual work belongs to today.

There is an important parallel between my friend's experience with sobriety and forgiveness. Many of us have experienced letting go of a hurt or a betrayal. We were relieved of the burden of resentment and felt released from the chains of old memories. Letting go is a great experience. And yet, many of us were also reminded, sometime down the road, of those old wounds, and to our surprise and perhaps even horror, old feelings of hurt and anger welled up from somewhere in our hearts. This tells us something important about forgiving others: rarely is forgiveness like an on/off switch. We cannot flip a switch and make all the hurt and resentment go away. Forgiving is an activity that takes time; it is not a mental decision. When we forgive, we learn to live with the people who have hurt us. Some of these people will be contrite; others will be wholly unrepentant.

Even if the person who hurt you dies, you live with his or her memory. Forgiveness involves learning to live with our memories in a loving way. That bears a little explanation. We forgive because forgetting is usually not an option. God designed us to remember. Memory is what gives us a personal identity and a shared story with the people we love; it is crucial to our senses of self and our deepest relationships. This is one reason that Alzheimer's Disease is so devastating. It robs the patient of memory and ravages the shared dimension of relationships.

Forgiveness is, in part, a way of remembering. We begin by remembering who we are. I am a person who needs and receives mercy. I may have done nothing to warrant the evil done to me, but I am deeply aware of my own myriad failings and of the new life Jesus gave me on the cross. Remembering who we are helps us to see those who injured us as people just like us. They need mercy; Christ died for them as well (Matthew 18:23–35). Remembering our own need for mercy and acknowledging how much we resemble the very people who hurt us will not immediately erase our hurt, nor guarantee feelings of tenderness toward them. In fact, the work of forgiveness happens precisely when we are hurting and want to spit in someone else's eye.

Many writers claim that forgiveness heals us. Maybe it does. I think it is safer to say that failing to forgive will poison us, and that forgiveness has to take place before healing can occur. Forgiveness takes time. Struggling with it, day by day, is not a mark of failure. Persevering in the struggle to forgive is a sign that you are becoming something new: a forgiving person.

Repeat Offenders

In the criminal justice system, a repeat offender faces harsher punishment than a first-time offender. Previous convictions and imprisonments failed to produce any change in the criminal's behavior. Now, we can't see into other people's hearts, and Jesus taught us very clearly to steer clear of judging the state of someone else's soul. Nevertheless, we can see from someone's pattern of behavior that he or she is committed to a certain way of life. To use churchy language, you can tell when somebody is unrepentant.

It is difficult to say which is more galling. Some people repeatedly hurt others in exactly the same ways after saying, "I'm sorry." Others keep dishing out insult and injury without the slightest hint of remorse. Surely people like this don't deserve our forgiveness! Contrary to what many people suggest about Christian teaching, that is exactly right. They do not deserve forgiveness. No one deserves forgiveness. Forgiveness is a free gift. Mercy gives rise to forgiveness.

Nothing drives this point home more soundly than this key exchange between Peter and Jesus: "Then Peter came and said to him, 'Lord, if another member of the church sins against me, how often should I forgive? As many as seven times?' Jesus said to him, 'Not seven times, but, I tell you, seventy-seven times'" (Matthew 18:21–22). Apply Jesus' words to the repeat offenders in your life. Maybe someone in your family stiffed you in settling an inheritance, and has no intention of making things right. Perhaps you have a boss who makes jokes at your expense, a neighbor who spreads lies about you, or a loved one who will not stop drinking or gambling. Perhaps someone in your family simply refuses to carry his or her own weight with chores and caring for the kids. Even if they apologize, you know they are not really sorry. They keep doing the same old thing, over and over. Surely they do not deserve forgiveness?

As I said, unrepentant repeat offenders do not deserve forgiveness due to their own merit. Rather, followers of Jesus seek to forgive the unrepentant and the insincerely repentant because Jesus teaches us to forgive them. He does not say that forgiveness will restore an obviously broken relationship. I will say more about this later, as well as distinguishing between forgiveness and reconciliation. For now, let's stick to the idea that forgiveness is an act of mercy.

All forgiveness begins with our own admission that we have not kept the moral law. I myself am a repeat offender. Jesus died on the cross to give me the free gift of mercy, a forgiveness that I did not and could not earn. Jesus teaches us that recipients of mercy are finally free to be merciful people. We do not have to wait for someone else's contrition before refusing to let their behavior define our state of mind. We can let it go, and move on. It is not who someone is or what he or she has done that makes it possible to let go. On the contrary, we can let go of our resentments and grievances because of who *we* are (or who we long to be) in Jesus Christ. So, does this mean that Christians are doormats or masochists, that we let others abuse us at their will? Hardly! To paraphrase Lewis Smedes, just because you forgive someone doesn't mean you have to give him his job back. This brings us to the difference between forgiveness and reconciliation.

It's Not the Same

"It's just not the same." You may have said this about an old friendship, or even a marriage. You and someone you love went through a tough time. The relationship dissolved or came very close to coming apart at the seams. Over time, you have been able to patch things up, but the ease and transparency of your former conversations is now but a memory. Neither of you impulsively picks up the phone for a chat, or enthusiastically thinks about what you might do together next. There is effort where once you felt drawn by desire.

When we forgive someone, we free ourselves from the burden of resentment and bitterness about old wounds. But our forgiveness does not automatically restore those relationships. If you have ever mourned a lost or diminished relationship, you have discovered that forgiveness alone is not sufficient. Jesus certainly teaches us to forgive, and it bears much good fruit when we do. God created us for relationship: a relationship with him and relationships with each other. We are sons and daughters of God by adoption, through Jesus Christ. That makes us brothers and sisters through that same Jesus Christ. God the Father is not content with gathering a dysfunctional family, neither should followers of Jesus settle for a squabbling, fractious family. We are given a clear mission: Christ sends us to announce and to facilitate the greatest reweaving of relationships the world will ever see. As the apostle Paul said, "All this is from God, who reconciled us to himself through Christ, and has given us the ministry of reconciliation; that is, in Christ God was reconciling the world to himself, not counting their trespasses against them, and entrusting the message of reconciliation to us. So we are ambassadors for Christ, since God is making his appeal through us" (2 Corinthians 5:18–20).

Christ's love for us stirs a desire for relationship that will not be satisfied by our merely forgiving and then walking away. We will yearn not only for a healed soul but a restored relationship. In this life, however, our yearning for reconciliation will not be completely met. Reconciliation requires contrition. If you have hurt me or betrayed me or stolen from me, I will understandably keep my distance until I see that you have no intention of continuing the same behavior.

Some people will refuse to admit that they were wrong; they will show no remorse. Their posture prevents reconciliation from occurring. And yet, their refusal to be contrite should not extinguish our hope, because we can still trust that God is working relentlessly. We can respond to such situations by maintaining healthy boundaries, offering persistent prayer, and refusing to give up on God's power to restore the ones he loves. Even when genuine contrition is offered, it takes time, risk, and patience to reweave broken relationships. Restoring trust is slow, gradual work, and trust is the key ingredient for reweaving fractured bonds of affection.

Reconciliation does not press some kind of reset button on a relationship. The bond can never again be exactly what it was before it was broken. But strains and fractures in a relationship will not always result in diminished bonds. On the contrary, forgiveness and reconciliation, by the grace of God, bring us to a deeper, more mature connection. God reconnects the scattered dots of human brokenness with the healing love of the cross of Christ. This is why St. Paul said, "If anyone is in Christ, he is a new creation" (2 Corinthians 5:17). Our fractured relationships will not be the same. Christ is making them into something more than we could make for ourselves. This is the hope we find in the cross.

Chapter Seven

Fear and Hope

Followers of Jesus live hope-inspired lives. This is not to say that we have successfully developed the habit of positive thinking or that we are optimistic by nature. In fact, hope is not a human achievement at all. Hope is a gift that comes as the result of a relationship with Jesus. The clearest example I have is from John's gospel. On the day of Jesus' resurrection, he appeared to his disciples. He showed them his hands and feet so they would know that he was the crucified and risen Lord. Then he breathed on them and said, "Receive the Holy Spirit" (John 20:22). With the Father, Jesus breathes the Holy Spirit into each of his disciples. He literally inspires us.

The word "inspire" is derived from the Latin word *inspirare*, and it means "to breathe in." "Spirit" and "breath" come from the same root in Latin (*spirare*), as well as in Greek (*pneuma*) and in Hebrew (*ruach*). Therefore, it is no surprise that the Bible leads us to connect the idea of the Spirit with the image of God's breath. When we follow Jesus, we breathe in his spirit. The Holy Spirit changes our hearts, empowers us, and sustains us. "I am the vine; you are the branches. Whoever abides in me and I in him, he it is that bears much fruit, for apart from me you can do nothing" (John 15:5). When we follow Jesus, he abides in us. We draw strength, direction, and purpose from him. Jesus inspires us by giving us the Holy Spirit as a guarantee that he is already at work connecting the dots of our lives. As Paul said, "In him you also, when you heard the word of truth, the gospel of your salvation, and believed in him, were sealed with the promised Holy Spirit, who is the guarantee of our inheritance until we acquire possession of it" (Ephesians 1:13–14).

And yet, deeply faithful Christians struggle with fear, the nagging feeling that life will fall apart in some way. Opportunities to be afraid or to worry present themselves to us every day. Parenting scares us to death. We worry that we will not be able to protect our children from bullies, sex offenders, or Internet brain rot. And even if we do keep them safe, we might fail to provide the particular dance class, sports team, summer camp, article of clothing, music lesson, or cultural exposure that will ensure their happiness and success. A perennial fear is running out of what we need, not having enough to retire, to send the kids to college, to take care of ourselves in extreme old age, or to just pay the bills this month.

Some people develop the habit of imagining the worst-case scenario of every situation. They are always waiting for the other shoe to drop. The other shoe could be a national or even global calamity. The national debt threatens to wipe us all out. Global warming is destroying the planet. (I am not denying either of these things, just pointing out how obsessive we can be about them.) Fear can become very personal. We dread that we will not matter, we will be rejected, we will not measure up, we will fail, we will be found out as the frauds we are, or we will be crushed by the challenges we face.

No wonder the Bible tells us repeatedly not to fear. Fear robs us of the joy for which God designed us. That joy derives from the hope that God will reliably connect the dots of our lives. Fear is the suspicion that those dots will never really connect, or that the connections we do see are merely fleeting. When we assume fear as a habitual spiritual posture, we walk around as if some powerful, invisible hand is poised to reduce our lives to a heap of disconnected, hopelessly chaotic dots. Without the hope of arriving at some final coherence and significance, our motivation ebbs, and the sweetness of life turns to drudgery and even despair. At the foundation of all kinds of fear is the nagging feeling that nothing ultimately matters, that everything we seek to achieve will eventually be undone, and that all our loves and losses and triumphs and sacrifices will be erased by the impersonal passage of time.

If the Bible merely ordered us to stop worrying, its repeated warnings against fear would be completely unhelpful. This kind of commandment would be like telling an accident victim to stop bleeding, without treating the wound. Of course, the Bible does more than this. It diagnoses the cause of our fears and offers us a path toward liberation.

The Big Lie

Hope defies fear. Holy Scripture teaches this repeatedly. Notice that I said that hope *defies* fear; hope and fear are not mutually exclusive. They can and do wrestle with each other for dominance in our hearts and minds. Given the popularity of books that offer easy steps to spiritual success, you may be expecting me to offer you a list of things to do in your life that will erase fear and replace it with unadulterated hope. But you will be either relieved or disappointed to hear that I am not going to do that. This chapter does not belong on the self-help shelves at Barnes and Noble. Don't get me wrong. Hope grows within us when we make a habit of the age-old spiritual disciplines of prayer, Bible study, fasting, works of mercy, and the like. But it is important to see even these disciplines as ways of developing our relationship with our maker and Redeemer. He is the one who provides the help that we need.

A fruitful first step to resisting fear is asking a question so obvious that one might fail to ask it at all. Why are we so susceptible to fear? Evolutionary biologists, among others, point to how valuable fear is to survival. Hungry lions and raging fires frighten us because they could kill us. Fear prevents us from becoming human toast for a lion. However, it is not this realistic response to obvious, impending danger that we are talking about. The fear that siphons joy from our lives is like a pernicious computer virus, infecting one experience after another. The fear I have in mind is not the kind that drives us to run from the hungry lion down the street. Instead, it is the kind that keeps us up late at night, wondering how sad we will be when some hungry lion eats the children we might have someday. It is not fear in the face of obvious danger. We can adopt fearfulness as a habitual, almost preemptive response to the world around us. Why are we susceptible to worrying about not have enough when we earn more than an entire African village? Why do we worry that our adorable toddler may not marry the man of her dreams years from now?

Our struggle with fear begins with the "Big Lie." In the garden of Eden, the serpent persuaded Eve to eat the fruit of the Tree of the Knowledge of Good and Evil by telling her the lie that remains lodged in our hearts to this day, that God makes big promises, but he will not come through for us. The serpent said, "For God knows that when you eat from it your eyes will be opened, and you will be like God, knowing good and evil" (Genesis 3:5). In other words, he was telling Eve, "God promises that he will connect the dots, but we know that this is not true. Making sense of your life, justifying your existence, and making sure that what you do matters is completely up to you. Only you can connect the dots of your life, and it is entirely within your power."

You do not have to read this story literally to see its startling truth. Counting on God to connect the dots is easier said than done. The Big Lie is that God is not reliable, or that he does not genuinely care, or that he is not capable. Leaning on him gets you nothing except, perhaps, a brief period of mental anesthesia. You have to look out for yourself. The Big Lie gets plenty of traction. Just look at the price so many of us pay for career success, social status, and fame. People pursue these things doggedly, believing in vain that they will connect the dots for us.

Hope begins to take the power away from fear when we start entertaining the idea that we are victims of a lie. Contrary to the demonic murmuring in the dark corners of our soul, God is capable and reliable. He can and will connect the dots. Hope gains an even greater place in our hearts when we recognize that our feelings do not always accurately report the truth about things. When fear presses in, the mind can become a silent backseat passenger, not even a backseat driver. But God gave us minds so we could see the truth, even through the fog of anxiety.

Simply repeating to ourselves that God will come through for us because he dearly wants to give us unfettered joy will not dissolve fear like a waved magic wand would. Reiterating this truth to ourselves will banish fear for a season. But in a sense, the liar who told us this whopper in the first place has merely been cunning enough to stop talking for a while. When an opportune time arises, he will again e-mail or text us a simple message to undermine our confidence. If we start to respond, then the liar will call us in the middle of the night for interminable, anxiety-laden conversations. The difficult first step is to remind ourselves that we are dealing with a persistent lie, and to develop the habit of focusing on the truth, no matter how we may happen to feel. It is also important to distinguish real hope from its counterfeit.

Real Hope

Natalie was only nineteen, and an only child. Every Friday after work, Natalie drove ninety miles to visit her boyfriend. This made her mother a little jumpy. It was the return trip that drove her mother's blood pressure through the roof. Natalie never started the Sunday ride home before midnight. Each week, her mother would endure visions of highway carnage until Natalie walked in the door. Natalie came to see me about what she thought was her mother's unreasonable attitude. She said something like, "I don't know what she's so upset about. I believe in Jesus. He wouldn't let anything happen to me." Clearly Natalie had missed the bit about Christian martyrs in her history lessons.

Hope liberates us from fear. But false hope is a spiritual car wreck waiting to happen. Natalie's story illustrates for us a common misconception about hope. Natalie assumes that faith in Jesus protects her from harm, danger, and suffering. What she calls hope is based on a transaction she believes she has made with God: if I believe in Jesus, God will guarantee me the future I want. As a reward for my faith, God owes me good things; his end of the bargain is to protect me from danger, disappointment, and failure.

Natalie wanted to visit her boyfriend. She believed that God's supernatural protection gave her a pass from all the obvious dangers of late-night driving on mountain roads. Her version of hope let her dispose of common sense and prudence. She presumed that she could take unreasonable risks because God owed her one.

Let me make a few things clear. Natalie really did have a sincere, if naïve, faith. I had the common sense to stay out of the triangle between Natalie and her mom. And no, "Natalie" is not a pseudonym for my daughter.

Now let's get back to hope and its counterfeit. If hope actually conformed to Natalie's view of things, then we would all be in for a bad time. God would inevitably let us down. Whether or not we have faith in Christ, each one of us will know disappointment, frustration, sorrow, and pain. As Jesus said, "For he makes his sun rise on the evil and on the good, and sends rain on the just and on the unjust" (Matthew 5:45). Life does not suddenly become fair or untroubled if you are a follower of Jesus. Thanks be to God, Natalie's view of hope was not accurate. What is real hope?

Genuine hope lies in what Jesus actually promises. His resurrection promises us new life: new life on this side of the grave and a new heaven and earth when he comes again. For now, let's set aside life after this life and concentrate on what the resurrection means for us. You may at one time or another have heard someone sincerely say, "My life is ruined." Sometimes we come to places where we can't see any way forward. A child dies. A loved one endures terrible illness. We experience bitter divorce, public scandal, financial collapse, diminished health, or career failure.

Jesus does not promise to prevent such things, as if through magic (although the Lord does sometimes intervene miraculously. Why he does sometimes but not other times is a topic for another time). Rather, his resurrection ensures us that these hardships will not be the last word. Sometimes hope means his giving us the power to endure what we thought would crush us. "Let us run with endurance the race" (Hebrews 12:1). Without the support of Christ, suffering and sorrow may end in despair, bitterness, or cynicism. In contrast, Christ's resurrection promises us new life after we pass through the valley of the shadow of death. The new life is not less, but more than the existence we knew before encountering heartbreak, failure, betrayal, or any of the other things we dread. Jesus does not heedlessly send us trials and suffering to make us grow, but he does use them as an occasion to nurture us toward eternal life.

The apostle Paul wrote, "And we know that in all things God works for the good of those who love him, who have been called according to his purpose" (Romans 8:28 NIV). By God's grace, a broken heart does not stop beating. Neither does it labor from beat to beat, yearning to be done with life. Instead, the power of the resurrection makes a broken heart bolder in its courage and more tender in its capacity to love. In God's hands, patience, perseverance, understanding, wisdom, peace, joy, love, and kindness are the fruits of life's changes and chances. This is the hope that gains the upper hand over fear.

Now, let's look at how to avail ourselves of genuine hope by looking at a particular source of worry: our children. Our worry as parents is a specific kind of fear that instructs us about how fear in general works and how hope acts to free us from fear's grip.

Will the Kids Be Okay?

Our oldest son Andrew is now in his mid-twenties. He bench presses over 300 pounds and serves in the United States Marines as a corpsman. Along with his pals on deployment, he has unflinchingly eaten things that I pay exterminators to kill and call animal control to capture. He does not need a firearm to be a dangerous weapon. And yet, I worry about him.

My worry is not, perhaps, based on what you'd think. Joy and I do not dwell on the possibility of another deployment. Visions of Afghanistan, IEDs, and radical insurgents do not keep me up late at night. Different matters tug at my heart. Is he happy? What will his career path be? Will he have a happy marriage? Will he continue to grow in his faith, finding strength, comfort, joy, and guidance in his relationship with Christ?

The worrying started all the way back in Andrew's infancy. Leaving the hospital, when we strapped him into the car seat for the first time, I was gripped by the realization that I was responsible for properly caring for, guarding, guiding, and nurturing this little guy. I was so cautious in my driving that day that the normally ten-minute car ride home seemed to take an hour. Sitting in the back with Andrew, Joy asked me, "Why are you driving so slowly?"

"There's group of runners in the road in front of me," I said.

About half an hour later, she noticed that I had stopped. "What's the holdup?"

"I caught up to the runners again."

We worry about what will happen to our kids. We worry about our adequacy as mothers and fathers. Some parents respond to this worry with crushing hypervigilance, accurately called helicopter parenting. They hover over every aspect of their kids' lives, hoping to prevent the worst from happening and to ensure that their kids will have only happy, rewarding experiences, and all the best opportunities. At the opposite extreme, some parents are so afraid of alienating their sons and daughters that they assume a permissive posture. These parents do not set boundaries because they want their children to see them as friends. They misconstrue caring as undiscerning acceptance. Love wins, as it were.

There is another attitude for parenting. "Jesus said, 'Let the little children come to me'" (Matthew 19:14). Three-times-distressed parents sought Jesus' healing for their children, and Jesus healed them each time. Read the stories of Jarius's daughter (Mark 5:22), the Canaanite woman (Matthew 15:22), and the father with the boy tormented by seizures (Mark 9:24). Each of these passages teaches us a range of things, but they also teach us about how hope overcomes the fears we have about our children. Jesus teaches us to place them in his care.

Before you roll your eyes at the simplicity of this passage, let me tell you how I myself experienced its truth, and what it actually means. Just when my daughter Meredith was learning to pull herself up and take her first tentative steps, we discovered that she had a hole in her heart, and she needed open heart surgery. Coronary surgeons might think of this as routine, but this was my daughter we were talking about. Joy and I were sorely afraid that Meredith might die. A priest recommended to me that I pray each day to Jesus, and imagine myself handing Meredith over to him. In the midst of one of these prayers, I snatched her back and said, "No! You might not give her back!" I do not generally hear voices, but I heard one at that moment. It may not have been audible outside of my own head, but it was clear. Christ said, "When you give her to me, you give her to life itself."

Jesus was not offering me a guarantee that Meredith would be miraculously healed, nor even a promise that the surgery would go without a hitch. Instead, with his simple words, he invited me to see parenting in a new light. Meredith was God's before she was ever mine. He entrusted her to me so that I might know the great joy of joining Him in nurturing, guiding, and caring for her. His risk in trusting me was unimaginable. As much as I love my daughter, his love for her infinitely exceeds mine.

My fears about my children recede when I remember whose they are. The death and resurrection of Jesus Christ does not exempt them from the changes and chances of this life. Neither do the cross and the empty tomb ensure that my own heart will never be broken as a father.

The mystery of the crucified and risen Christ reassures me that love has the last word, not sorrow or pain or tragedy. Love will connect the dots, even when what I fear the most seems poised to erase every line that joins the dots into a coherent picture. Hope takes the upper hand in our lives when we remember that Christ is already at the bottom of things, connecting the dots even when appearances lead us to believe the opposite.

Getting to the Bottom of Things

As a younger man, I served on a on the faculty of a college philosophy department. Although I enjoyed doing research and teaching advanced courses, my real love was teaching introductory classes. Freshmen entered those classrooms with a willingness to engage in big questions that got to the very bottom of things. They were not being flip or ironic when they asked, "What is the meaning of life?" It was thrilling to watch their eyes light up with discovery, hope, and bold vision.

That was a different time. Although I know many young people who still sincerely wrestle with what makes their lives significant and what greater purpose their lives might serve, I am also seeing something else these days. Cynicism has become the mark of sophistication. Scoffing at the idea that life has a larger meaning seems more intellectually respectable than searching for some source of meaning beyond ourselves. For many people today, there is no reliable bottom of things. Rob Bell expresses this better than I can: "Cynicism is the new religion of our world. Whatever it is, this religion teaches that it isn't as good as it seems. It will let you down. It will betray you. That institution? That church? That politician? That authority figure? They'll all let you down. Whatever you do, don't get your hopes up. Whatever you think it is, whatever it appears to be, it will burn you, just give it time" (Bell, "It's Not Christmas Yet").

This cynical posture is tenable only as long as nothing matters to you yet. But once you have invested yourself in a family, a career, a community, or a movement, then the world according to the religion of cynicism is a horrifying place to dwell. Anybody who has been around the block at least a couple of times knows that life is always threatening to fly apart at the seams. Things often fail to go as planned; sometimes they go frighteningly wrong. We get through those times because we have some sense that life will turn right side up in the end. The dots will eventually connect. But the religion of cynicism claims that it will all eventually break apart. As William Butler Yeats famously wrote in his poem "The Second Coming," "Things fall apart; the centre cannot hold." This fear has nagged humans since the beginning—or at least since the fall. Satan murmurs it in our ears: "God will let you down in the end." There is no bottom to things. Nothing connects the dots.

Slipping into the clutches of this fear is the darkness that the Light of the World comes to dissolve. The incarnation of the living God in the man Jesus Christ gives us proof, in the flesh, that the religion of cynicism is but a phony bill of goods. The apostle John said, "In the beginning was the Word" (John 1:1). That is the familiar translation. But here it is retranslated: "At the bottom of things, there is meaning." Translators usually render the Greek word *arche* as "beginning," but it also means "at the root of things," "at the foundation," or "at the bottom of things." What we read as "Word" in the familiar translation is the Greek word *logos*, a rich term that can express "news," "logic," or, as I suggest here, "meaning." And so, the apostle John is telling us that the Son of God is at the very bottom of things, connecting everything. He is the alpha and the omega, the beginning and the end. In Christ, it all hangs together. All the dots connect.

It is easy for many of us to imagine God the Father as a distant designer. He draws up blueprints and makes plans about how things should work, but seems awfully far away. In truth, God the Son gets inside of things. In Jesus Christ, God insinuated himself right into the middle of the messy muddle we call life. Jesus acts as the glue that holds things together, especially after they have broken and threaten to crumble into pieces. The funny thing about glue is that we do not see it at work, and yet it binds together different and various parts into a beautiful, elegant whole.

The Son of God has come to dwell in our midst, not merely alongside us, but right in the heart of all that we do, at the very center of our lives. Because the Son of God himself comes to dwell among us, we can persevere through every challenge and endure even the most piercing heartaches, because we know that his love is already making things whole. When we get to the bottom of things, we find that Jesus Christ has been dwelling there all along, connecting the dots before we even noticed it. The problem, of course, is that he seems to be taking his sweet time about finishing. In the meantime, we have to live, while so many of dots remain unconnected.

Inspired by Hope in the Meantime

Anne Lamott tells a story about riding a ski lift. She intended to get off at the intermediate skiers' slope, but she failed to recognize the jump-off until the lift had already moved on. Lamott decided to leap off the moving lift, from a height of five or six feet. She did not soar like an eagle. She flapped to a crash-landing. To her relief, most people around pretended not to notice, and she waved away the few who came over to sympathize. Then the nausea hit. As she stood there on the verge of passing out, she prayed for Jesus to help her. "I don't know how long I stood there with my hand clamped to my mouth, only my poles and a frayed, consignment-store faith to support me. All I knew was that help is always on the way, a hundred percent of the time . . . I know that when I call out, God will be near, and hear and help eventually. Of course, it is the "eventually" that throws one into despair" (Lamott, *Grace (Eventually)*, 17–18).

At one point or another, each one of us has called out for help. Maybe it came as a momentary lapse in our usual calm when we realized that we could no longer see our toddler on the beach, or when we discovered that we had had food in our teeth through an entire interview, or when we got really bad news. Help! We felt it in our guts before we even thought it. Life has taught us not to ask for help out loud. Calling out for help betrays the awful secret that we are not as composed and in control as we pretend to be, as we assume everyone else is, as we fear that God expects us to be before he decides to invite us to dinner. In a way, calling for help is the beginning of hope. But then we discover that God was already on the way before the first butterfly even took flight in our stomachs.

There are times when help comes with miraculous speed; the threat or challenge dissolves as quickly as it came. Jesus turns on his nightlight of the world and banishes the shadow that make us cower under the covers. But sometimes, Jesus only comes to our help eventually. Adversity, sorrow, conflict, or suffering persist. It can feel as though

God is not listening, or does not care, or maybe cannot help after all. Lamott has it right: the spiritual challenge in relying on God hits home when we experience firsthand that he comes to help *eventually*. How do we keep going in the meantime, between the cry for help and God's rescue? How do we live with that divine "eventually?" How do we cope with the urgency of our longing and God's patient, even dawdling sense of timing?

It turns out that the gap between our cries for help and God's final rescue is where Jesus does some of his best work. That gap is the territory of hope. The prophet Isaiah was responding to exactly this kind of spiritual challenge when he said, "They who wait for the Lord shall renew their strength; they shall mount up with wings like eagles" (Isaiah 40:31). Let's look a little more closely at Isaiah's words and what was happening in the lives of the Israelites when he said them.

The Israelites were in the midst of the Babylonian captivity. The Babylonians had conquered Jerusalem, torn down its wall, and destroyed the temple. A large part of the population was then taken captive and deported over 500 miles to Babylon. In that foreign empire, the Israelites were surrounded by alien customs and reduced to servitude. Their religion, their traditions, and their very identity as the people of God were objects of constant scorn.

As awful as all of this was, the Israelites saw their captivity as a just punishment for their own unfaithfulness. Despite receiving repeated prophetic warnings to change their course, the Israelites despised the ways of God by trampling on the poor, offering phony worship, and relying on their own political conniving to save them. The results were catastrophic. Instead of inhabiting God's Promised Land, they lived as strangers in a godforsaken kingdom. The riches that God had heaped upon them now lined someone else's pockets. They had nobody to blame but themselves.

And yet, despite all of this, God promised to redeem them. God spoke words of comfort to the people even while they were in the grip of captivity. He would return them from exile, restore them to Jerusalem, rebuild the walls of the great city, and even build a new temple. he would come again and dwell in their midst. He would take them out of their misery and live with them as their God, and they would be his people. He was coming—eventually. Decades passed, and the Israelites were still in Babylon. Jerusalem was a distant heap of rubble. Despair threatened to set in. And this is when hope began to sustain them.

Sometimes we turn to God for help, and the truth of the matter is that we want him to fix things for us. We want a happier marriage, more compliant children, and understanding parents. We want our prognosis to improve, our financial prospects to look up, to find a friend or a spouse, and to not be so alone, afraid, or self-loathing. Help! We feel as though we are here and we want God to get us over there, to whisk us from Babylon to Jerusalem with a snap of his mighty finger; we want Him to fix it.

But inevitably, our problem runs deeper than we had thought. The ancient Israelites had much more than a geographical problem—and so do we. A celestial magician could easily solve a relocation issue with a wave of his wand. But this isn't the problem; we need something more than a magician. We need the Redeemer. You see, if God had merely relocated the Israelites from Babylon to Jerusalem, then the very same hearts that had gotten them deported in the first place would again inhabit Jerusalem. All that old unfaithfulness that had gotten them in that fix would start up all over again. Big changes, such as changes of heart, mind, soul, will, and relationship, have to happen before a moving van will do any good. *Who* the Israelites were, and who *we* are, has to change before it makes a difference *where* we are. God will set things completely right eventually. In the meantime, God is not merely biding his time, turning his back, or sleeping at the wheel. Jesus works with us day by day to make all these changes in us before God's "eventually" can become a present reality.

You might be tempted to think that living in the meantime is full of toil, impatience, or drudgery, like waiting for the weekend, or Christmas, or summer vacation: trying really hard to be holy and righteous, and lugging around a sense of guilt and unworthiness. You might think that we trudge along, staying just one step ahead of despair at our own spiritual inadequacy. But that is not what Isaiah tells us. He says that we will soar on eagle's wings. Following Jesus means stretching out our wings and letting the Holy Spirit, the *ruach*, the very breath of God, bear us up to great heights and propel us along distances that mere human foot traffic could never achieve. In the meantime, hope lifts us up and carries us forward.

As we wait for God to complete his redeeming work, we learn to rely on God, to soar with hope instead of merely pushing through and plodding along. The maker of heaven and earth is with us, not just at the beginning of things or only at the finish line. He is with us in every routine moment in between. Our God is the Sovereign of the meantime. It is precisely in the midst of trial and adversity that we learn to stretch out our wings and trust in the updrafts of God's breath, and in his abiding Spirit, to support us, sustain us, and propel us forward to new life.

It may seem safer to slog along by our own power, to stay closer to the ground, to lean forward and push against the obstacles in our path. After all, many of us are afraid of spiritual heights. We fear that we might simply drop like stones. Some people who think they are following Jesus look at life as an exhausting hike of moral effort and spiritual exertion. They rely upon their own wills and their own spiritual disciplines and never learn to stretch out their wings and take flight by relying on the Spirit to carry them.

We who follow Jesus commit ourselves to living in the meantime. The cross and the empty tomb are behind us. The second coming and the new heaven and new earth are before us. We live between what Jesus *has* accomplished for us and what he *will* accomplish for us. Now we dwell in the meantime, where Jesus inspires us. To return to the central image of this book, our lives are like an incomplete connect-the-dots puzzle. We are always taking the next step without seeing the big picture. But we can take those steps boldly, and even joyfully, because we are inspired by the hope that in all things, Jesus Christ is connecting the dots.

About the Author

Jake Owensby is the Bishop of the Episcopal Diocese of Western Louisiana. Previously, Jake served as the Dean of St. Mark's Cathedral in Shreveport, Louisiana, and led congregations in Florida, Alabama, and Missouri. Before answering the call to ordained ministry, Jake was a philosophy professor who taught classes on the history of philosophy and on a variety of other introductory and advanced topics. Jake has been married to his wife, Joy, for almost thirty years. They have a daughter in college, a son in the US Marine Corps, a son in high school, and a golden retriever who enjoys a comfortable retirement. Alexandria, Louisiana, is their home.

BIBLIOGRAPHY

Arends, Carolyn. "Satan's a Goner." *Christianity Today*, http://www.christianitytoday.com /ct/2011/february/satansagoner.html (accessed February 2011).

Bell, Rob. *Love Wins.* New York: HarperCollins, 2011.

⎯⎯⎯. "It's Not Christmas Yet." *Relevant*, http://www.relevantmagazine.com/god/deeper-walk/features/27641-its-not-christmas-yet, (accessed December 20, 2011).

Boyd, Gregory A. *God of the Possible.* Grand Rapids: Baker Books, 2000.

⎯⎯⎯. *Is God to Blame?* Downers Grove, IL: InterVarsity, 2003.

Cary, Phillip. *Good News for Anxious Christians.* Grand Rapids: Brazos, 2010.

Chan, Francis, with Danae Yankoski. *Crazy Love.* Colorado Springs: David C. Cook, 2008.

Chan, Francis, with Preston Sprinkle. *Erasing Hell.* Colorado Springs: David C. Cook, 2011.

DeYoung, Kevin. *Just Do Something.* Chicago: Moody, 2009.

Galli, Mark. *God Wins.* Carol Stream, IL: Tyndale House, 2011.

Heimel, Cynthia. *If You Can't Live Without Me, Why Aren't You Dead Yet?* New York: Grove Press, 2002.

Keller, Timothy. *Counterfeit Gods.* New York: Dutton, 2009.

_____. *King's Cross.* New York: Dutton, 2011.

Lamott, Anne. *Grace (Eventually).* New York: Penguin Books, 2007.

Lewis, C. S. *The Four Loves.* New York: Harcourt Books, 1988.

McKnight, Scot. *One.Life.* Grand Rapids: Zondervan, 2010.

_____. *The King Jesus Gospel.* Grand Rapids: Zondervan, 2011.

Thomas, Oliver. *10 Things Your Minister Wants to Tell You.* New York: St. Martin's, 2007.

Wright, N. T. *Surprised by Hope.* New York: HarperCollins, 2008.

Made in the USA
Lexington, KY
05 June 2016